My Side of the Bridg

T0363747

Mary-Anne Gale is a research fellow at the University of South Australia. She has written many articles and chapters for academic publications on Aboriginal education issues, and is the author of the book *Dhangum Djorra'wuy Dhāwu: a history of writing in Aboriginal languages*. Her PhD, 'Poor Bugger Whitefella got no Dreaming', focused on the representation of Aboriginal Dreaming narratives as published texts, looking in particular at the writings of the Ngarrindjeri man David Unaipon.

Mary-Anne collaborated with the Kaurna Elder Uncle Lewis O'Brien in writing his autobiography, *And the Clock Struck Thirteen*, also published by Wakefield Press, 2007.

My Side of the Bridge

The life story of Veronica Brodie

as told to Mary-Anne Gale

Wakefield Press

I dedicate this book to my late sister Leila Rankine who was able to pass on to me the wisdom of the Ngarrindjeri culture. — V.B.

To my late dad, Max Gale, for his compassion. — M.G.

Wakefield Press
1 The Parade West
Kent Town
South Australia 5067

www.wakefieldpress.com.au

First published 2002
Reprinted 2007

Copyright © Veronica Brodie, 2002

Pelican illustration by Jonathon Inverarity
Cover design by Liz Nicholson, designBITE
Designed and typeset by Clinton Ellicott, Wakefield Press
Printed and bound by Hyde Park Press, Adelaide

National Library of Australia
Cataloguing-in-publication entry

Gale, Mary-Anne.
My side of the bridge: the life story of Veronica Brodie.

ISBN-13: 978 1 86254 557 1.
ISBN-10: 1 86254 557 X.

1. Brodie, Veronica. 2. Aborigines, Australian – Women – South Australia – Biography. 3. Narrinyeri (Australian people) – Biography. I. Title.

306.0899915

Government of South Australia

Arts SA

fox creek wines

Publication of this book has been assisted by Alison McDougall and Colin Telfer.

Contents

Preface

I first heard Auntie Veronica Brodie tell her story one evening in 1995, and from that moment I knew it had to be published. Veronica is a gifted story teller and orator and, more importantly, her story represents the experience of being a Nunga in South Australia. I had read many biographies that told the stories of Aboriginal people from different parts of Australia, including the South Australian collection *Women of the Centre*. But at the time there were no life stories of Aboriginal people from southern South Australia, particularly stories that were told in their own words. And there were certainly no published biographies emanating from the strong and proud Ngarrindjeri people, whose homeland centres around Raukkan on the shores of Lake Alexandrina.

Auntie Veronica also has Kaurna heritage, and it was this fascinating side of her story that I first heard that night nearly seven years ago. I already had a great interest in Indigenous Australian literature, having worked for many years in Aboriginal schools and been closely involved in the production of books in Aboriginal languages. But I also had an interest in the way Aboriginal people's stories are represented in books, and was concerned about the lack of opportunity Aboriginal people have to tell their own stories in their own words. It's hard to get published even if you are an accomplished writer, but even harder when your skills are in speaking and not writing. So with Veronica's skills as a story teller, and my determination to tell Veronica's story in her voice and not that of a white writer or editor, together we set about committing Veronica's remarkable, humorous and at times tragic story to paper.

Over the period of a year, I followed Veronica around to her many speaking engagements and recorded 'her story'. We also spent many hours at either her house, my house or relaxing down at the Gale family farm at Back Valley, near Victor Harbor, recording onto audio-tape the many different chapters of her life. I then transcribed all the tapes, word for word, to produce a very large oratory volume. From this I cut and pasted, and continuously consulted, until we eventually came up with a written manuscript. Some further editing has occurred on the way, particularly over the five years that the manuscript has passed backwards and forwards between Wakefield Press, myself and Veronica. Much has happened over this time, including a long and drawn out saga that has a lot to do with a bridge. But the story that lies before you in this book remains Veronica's story and it is still in her own words.

Mary-Anne Gale, 2002

Namawi rundi, mamaranggal,	Our friend, poor thing,
nginti pon-ur	you have passed away
Ngarni betulun mi:wi ngum-ambi	We are upset for you
Ngarni kaltun mi:w-angk*	We are in grief

On 3 May 2007 Auntie Veronica Brodie, the much loved and respected Elder of the Ngarrindjeri and Kaurna peoples, passed away at the age of 66 years. She was a true leader of her people in their struggles for justice, and an inspiration to anyone fortunate enough to meet her. May her spirit rest in peace with the Ancestors.

---

* A lament in the Ngarrindjeri language

Chapter 1

My Kaurna Heritage

I want you to imagine your way back to the year of 1840 on the Port Adelaide River. Just think what it would have looked like then. No buildings, just the natural trees, the grasses, the reeds, the black swans on the river, and the Kaurna camps that were there. The whole area was filled with traditional wurlies, with Kaurna people moving up and down. It would have been a wonderful sight in those days to stand on the hill and see all the campfires lit up all the way to the Outer Harbor. It would have been like fairyland.

All the land along the coast to Outer Harbor and along the Port River was Kaurna land. They call it Yerta Bulti, which means 'the land of the dead' or 'land of grief', because a lot of Kaurna people in this area died from the smallpox, which reached this area even before South Australia was officially made a colony. The virus came along the Murray River from the eastern states, and it wiped out a lot of Kaurna people in the Port Adelaide area. Then the Kaurna people took the brunt of the invasion of white man into the colony of South Australia. They lost everything, the whole lot.

My name is Veronica Brodie and I'm of Ngarrindjeri and Kaurna descent. I am Kaurna through my matrilineal descent line, because my mother's mother's mother, my great-grandmother, was a Kaurna woman from the Port River area. Her name was Lartelare Rebecca Spender and her land was at Glanville, near the river. Her daughter, Laura Glanville Harris, was my grandmother, and she was born on the site where the

1

CSR sugar factory once stood at Glanville. Her story is very sad, because it tells of her dispossession and of her removal by the government from that land.

Lartelare married my great-grandfather, George Spender, who was born at The Needles, which was a ration station near the Coorong – he was born in the old house there. My grandmother eventually married a Ngarrindjeri man, and so did my mother. My mother was Rebecca Harris, daughter of Laura Glanville Harris and Jacob Harris, who was a strong Ngarrindjeri man. So my mother was Kaurna on her mother's side and Ngarrindjeri on her father's side, but she talked to me of her Kaurna heritage.

Alf Spender, Grandmother's brother, told the anthropologist Norman Tindale in 1935 that his mother's sister was Ivaritji, who is well known among historians and was referred to as a Kaurna princess by many white people in Adelaide. Ivaritji referred to my great-grandmother, Lartelare, as her tribal sister.

My great-grandmother was the keeper of the black swans in the Port River. She often fed them and protected them so that men couldn't come and kill them. Today the Ngarrindjeri eat the black swan – that's a part of their food – but for the Kaurna it was a protected bird. So on my mother's side the black swan is my totem, and on my father's side the pelican is my totem.

Grandmother was proud to talk of her Kaurna background. Although she didn't tell a lot, the little that she did tell us was very interesting. Grandmother told us of many, many camps that were sited from Glanville all the way to Outer Harbor, and that's quite a big stretch. As a little girl, she visited the camps along the coast with her mother and father, and with other family members who were camping around. And they also often walked to the River Torrens to see relatives camped along there.

Grandmother loved it at Glanville because they were never far from the ocean. They'd go down and walk into the water at Semaphore and catch fish and cook it on the reeds. The reeds were placed on top of a fire, and they'd make a damper in the ashes. What better way to eat? They had good hunting around there, good food. And so life on this peninsula meant a lot to the Kaurna people.

Down where the road bridge goes across the Causeway is where the Port River ends, and that's where Aboriginal people used to corroboree. They also would sit there and wait for the boats to come in. The drums they used to play were made out of possum skin. The Kaurna were well known for their possum-skin drums, but they also used the skins to make clothing and footwear. Even the material they used to cover their wurlies was possum skin. They used to eat a lot of possum too.

There were mangroves down at Glanville and Port Adelaide before the wharves were built. Those mangroves were a source of food for the Kaurna people who lived there. They used to take lobsters out of the Port River. Grandmother also told me they used to get shellfish – mussels and oysters. There were black swans too (which we didn't eat because he was protected) and they used to catch birds and fish.

With the Kaurna, when somebody died, they buried them and then just moved on, and they also buried all their things with them. They had a number of burial sites at Glanville, so they didn't have a long way to carry the dead – they were always within a short distance. You know, it's quite scary to think how many bones are out there. And how many more burial sites have been covered by buildings? Over the years they must have dug up hundreds of bones.

There's a burial ground just around the corner from my house at Largs Bay, on the south-east corner of Largs Bay Primary School, half-way between the school fence and the street. This old fella came and told me once, 'I was six years old and they were digging up these bones.' He said he was peeping from behind the wall at the school, and he was saying to this older boy, 'What's going on there?' And the older boy said, 'They're digging up some bones.' It was an Aboriginal burial ground. The kids at the school were told they weren't allowed to go near that spot. And this old fella told me that there were three bodies, and they eventually transplanted the bones to another burial site just outside of the school yard. He said, 'My mate and I peeped around and we watched them do it. They pulled all the bones out and covered them over with something and then just put them back in there. They crushed them all down and then packed them in with dirt and whatever.' They're still there today, as far as I know.

I believe you can live on a burial ground, but only if it is a peaceful one. My late sister Leila Rankine lived in Mitchell Park, and she lived on a burial ground right up until she died, but she said she felt peaceful about living there. My sister had Kaurna heritage, so she was able to live with the spirits there.

The big reserve opposite the naval base at Gawler Reach, just past the Birkenhead Bridge, is the site of the biggest Kaurna burial ground in the area. They put a reserve over the top of it – Birkenhead Reserve – which is quite a big reserve, but the burial ground is still there. They were even talking about digging tunnels under the ground for kids to crawl through. But there are burial grounds under there!

I read in a book that there's a stretch of road in Loxton that's made out of the crushed skulls of Aboriginal people. They dug the bones up when they were building the road, and instead of burying them they crushed them up and put them in the road mix. That shocked the daylights out of me.

Another part of our history is the water wells. Grandmother Glanville said there were clear freshwater wells running right through the area around Glanville and Semaphore, where the local Kaurna people camped. The water was absolutely pure and clear. These wells were just dug out of the dunes. Many of the wells in the Port area have dried up, because they were only there when the Kaurna people were around. But the local council has built some walkways through the Ray Marten Reserve to protect the water wells there from being destroyed. You can walk there and see where the wells once were. There are many good things happening now that the history of the Kaurna people has started to come back to Port Adelaide.

*

Not much is known about the Kaurna people, because their history was a closed history. But the history of the Kaurna is now coming to light. We are at last beginning to be able to identify where our people come from. That's important to us. People are starting to realise that Port Adelaide has a black history, and they just have to accept it – and they should also respect it. It's the history of that land that makes it so beautiful. This is where the Kaurna Dreaming Ancestor Tjilbruke once travelled, right through to Outer Harbor.

Now Tjilbruke was an Ibis man from the other side of the Port River, opposite where the Emu people used to be. The emu is very sacred to the Kaurna people. The Dreaming story of Tjilbruke tells of how his nephew, Kulultuwi, was speared because he killed an emu. You see, he took the life of something that was very precious to the Kaurna people. When Tjilbruke heard this, he went to get his nephew's body. He then carried his beloved nephew all the way from Marion along the Fleurieu Peninsula right down to Cape Jervis, where he placed his body in a cave. On the way down the coast Tjilbruke wept for his nephew, and his tears formed many of the springs along the Tjilbruke trail.

Georgina Williams formed the Tjilbruke committee some years ago and my sister Leila and I helped mark out the

Dreaming track of the story of Tjilbruke. Cairns have been placed to mark the spots where Tjilbruke sat and cried as he held Kulultuwi, his nephew whom he loved so dearly. You can follow that Dreaming trail all the way down. Every time I do the trail I find something I missed the last time.

And the Kaurna language is also being learnt today. It started with a couple of words at the Aboriginal Community College, but now those couple of words have gone to many, many words, and we can learn a lot more ourselves from the grammar and word-lists left by the Lutheran missionaries, Teichelmann and Schürmann, in 1840. Rob Amery, a linguist who specialises in the Kaurna language, is fitting words to songs that he's translated into Kaurna such as 'Three Little Mice'. When I first heard it in the Kaurna language, I thought it was just beautiful. Now the Kaurna language is being learnt by children at Kaurna Plains school, as well as by year 11 and 12 students at Inbarendi College and students at university. Thanks to Rob and Auntie Cherie Watkins and others, this language will go on, and I hope that the students now learning Kaurna will be able to carry the language further.

Tjilbruke was a Dreaming man, and if you do want to learn the Kaurna Aboriginal language I believe you must be able to understand the Dreaming stories that are told, because it's the Dreaming that keeps us going as Aboriginal people. Like the whiteman has his Bible, even if we believe in God too, our Dreaming is our religion. You see, there's two circles. Whiteman had a circle that only went so far, but Blackman, his circle went right round and it was complete. Our culture stayed in this Dreaming circle. And what's in that circle helps us to live our lives – it helps us to cope with our everyday living. This was told to my sister Leila, and she passed it on to me.

We are a people with a struggle, and bringing back our language is like bringing back gold. We're hoping our children today, our Aboriginal kids, will be able to learn the language and carry it on. We've each got our own language. You've got West Coast people in Adelaide, and you've got Pitjantjatjara people from the north, and you've got people from over the border and in the eastern States – they've all got their different languages. But we need a language for the Adelaide people; we need to know the language of the Adelaide Plains people, and that's the Kaurna language. And once that's spoken in almost every Aboriginal home in Adelaide, we'll be able to say, 'We've got a language.' And if we learn it well with our friends and families, then it may be the means of reconciliation, who knows?

My daughter Margaret did a tourism course at Tauondi, the Aboriginal Community College in the Port. She learnt the Kaurna language and culture. We hope one day she will be able to run tours about the local Kaurna people. Those sorts of tours, and educating people about the history of Adelaide, will help bring about understanding and reconciliation between whites and local Nunga people.*

And for me to hear the young people singing songs in Kaurna the way they do, and speaking the language, makes me feel very proud. I am only just now learning my mother's and my grandmother's language, and about many other parts of my Kaurna heritage. It's been a real thrill for me to learn more of my heritage and to see our Kaurna history coming back.

*

I was brought up on Ngarrindjeri land, at Raukkan on Lake Alexandrina. When I was growing up, I often asked my mother's mother, 'Grandmother, where did you come from?' because Grandmother was very different from a lot of the other Ngarrindjeri women that lived at Raukkan. She was very fair, and taller than any of the women on the mission. She was a big woman.

---

* Nunga is a term of group identity used by local Aboriginal people in southern South Australia.

She talked to Mum and her other daughters in this language, and I knew it wasn't Ngarrindjeri. Even her mats, her arts and crafts were different. She'd make little pockets that were flat along one side to hang on the wall. Grandmother was very clever with her hands. She'd also make feather flowers, and reed baskets and mats. Her designs for her mats and her baskets were beautiful. And I'd say to her, 'Grandmother, where did you learn to make that?' And she replied, 'My people used to make these' – the Kaurna people from the other side of the Port River. Grandmother's bird was the ibis. She made my sister Leila a bouquet out of its feathers for her wedding.

Because she was different I often questioned her: 'Grandmother, who was your mother? Who was your father? Where were you born?' But she wouldn't say anything. Had she sat down and told us of her life, we might have had a whole book of it here today – we might have had all that history there. But she never said a word. I had to beg her to find out what I did.

She sat me down one day and she told me, 'One day I'll take you and show you where I was born. I'll also show you where my mother's camp once stood, and where many other Kaurna camps were in that area.'

My grandmother took me up to Glanville at the age of about eleven or twelve. She said, 'I'll show you the site where we were kicked off our land.' So my mother, my grandmother and myself went up to Glanville. We walked up the road to the wharf and onto that site. And she stood outside the CSR factory and she shook her fist at it, and she told us how much she hated it.

I said, 'Grandmother, why do you hate it so much?' And she said, 'You don't know what that factory did to our people. What those people did, it left us as nothing!' At that time I didn't understand what Grandmother was talking about, but I knew that for some reason she hated that factory.

As I got older, I was able to ask her again about that land. She explained that her mother's old campsite was where the Jervois Bridge is now, about midway across the bridge, where the Hawker River used to flow into the Port River. Lartelare's campsite was there. The site was flooded out when the river was widened, so she moved her campsite over to where the sugar factory was built. So that's the birthplace of Laura Glanville Spender.

There was a man by the name of Captain Hart who bought most of the land at Glanville in the early days of South Australia's colonisation. He looked after the Kaurna people down there very well – in employment, and where they camped. He was a sea captain, and he gave a lot of Aborigines work. In fact, my great-grandmother Lartelare used to walk regularly to Glanville Hall to work for Captain Hart's wife, Mary Glanville Hart, in the kitchen and laundry.

Glanville Hall was a very grand place. Imagine the balls they would have held, and all the socialites that used to mix there! Lartelare would have gone in and cleaned up after them. My grandmother also worked there with her mother and helped with the washing or whatever she had to do. Grandmother remembered all the big puffy dresses they used to wear.

Captain Hart gave work to other Kaurna people in his flour mill on the opposite side of the Port River. He also got work for them on the wood boats and the sugar boats. But little did we know that, while Captain Hart was doing good to the Kaurna down here, he was black-birding in the north of the country. He was selling black people on the black market up in Queensland, you know, and he sold Aboriginal people overseas. Many people ended up over there because of Captain Hart. It makes you realise why there are so many Aboriginal bodies buried over the other side of the world, and why Aboriginal remains have to be brought back for burials.

There were a lot of sand dunes around Glanville Hall in those days, and the story that the very old white people tell us is that Captain Hart used to love to sit and listen to the songs of the Aboriginal people. They'd be camped in the sand dunes around his place, having their corroborees. But now the dunes and the large grounds are a golf course.

Glanville Hall is a beautiful old place. It has quite a history, because it was once known as St Francis' Boys Home, which housed a lot of Aboriginal lads from interstate and the Northern Territory. John Moriarty and Charlie Perkins were two of the boys who were there. You can still see the signatures that were left on the wall by these boys.

There's a tower up the top where they used to go to have a look around Port Adelaide. Out the front of the hall you can see an old lamp-post, which is reputedly from London Bridge. Around the back of the hall is the old coach house, which is still standing. It's used by the Scouts these days. The coach house was actually built on a burial ground. There's also a big water well under the huge Moreton Bay fig tree that stands between the hall and the coach house. The Kaurna people used to get a lot of water from that well.

When my grandmother reached the age of fourteen years, the government sold or leased that land where Lartelare camped, because it was Crown land according to British law. They sold or leased it to the CSR company. CSR thought that the Glanville site would be a very convenient place to put a sugar factory, because it was on the Port River and the boats could come in and take their sugar away. My grandmother and her family had no papers to prove that the Glanville land was theirs. So what could they do? They had to get up and move. They had to carry what little they had and find somewhere else to camp.

So they walked from the Glanville site all the way to the city – Grandmother and her younger brother James, and Great-grandfather and Great-grandmother, and *her* older brother, Alf Spender. They walked to the East Parklands. The police arrested them there. You can go back to the police records, and you can see that in 1890 Laura was arrested in Adelaide with her mother and her father and her younger brother James Spender. That was after they were kicked off their land at Glanville, and had to walk through to Adelaide, begging for food, begging for money and whatever they could get.

They eventually headed for Victoria Square, which was a popular camping place for Aboriginal people – it is called Tarndanyangga by the Kaurna. That site by the Adelaide Post Office has been a meeting place for a very, very long time. Because it held a big camp in those days, my grandmother's family tried to get a spot there and put up another wurlie after they got kicked off their land at Glanville.

When they got there they said they had nowhere else to go and asked if they could stay. But Tarndanyangga was full, so they were told to move on south to the coast at Glenelg, to Colley Reserve on the foreshore, and join the camp there, which they did. So for a number of years Grandmother lived with her family at Glenelg. But the land at Glanville still meant a lot to them. Even during that time they came back to see what was happening. They didn't have a horse and cart, so they had to walk. And the anger always used to get the better of them. They used to go away feeling really bad about what had happened.

The police didn't like it when Aboriginal people stayed around Adelaide. They kept trying to get Grandmother and her family out of town. The police arrested them for being 'idle and disorderly', and then gave them twenty-four hours' notice to leave, but a month later they were back again.

Kaurna people were taken from Adelaide and shipped out to different missions such as Poonindie on Eyre Peninsula, or up to Point Pearce to the north, or to Raukkan (Point McLeay)

– wherever they could be sent. They had lost what was their land, and many of them just roamed around. Some went as far as Tasmania. Just a short time ago, I received a letter from a woman living at Ottoway, near Semaphore, who said her father's grandfather could remember the very last of the Kaurna people being shoved onto the trains at Semaphore and being taken away to live elsewhere. It's just like the Jews were shoved onto the trains in Germany – the Kaurna people were shoved on the trains at Semaphore and taken away in those old box cars.

Some years before they lost their land, Great-grandmother Lartelare and Great-grandfather George Spender had met Jacob Harris, who became Grandmother Laura's husband. From a young girl she was promised in marriage to him. Grandfather Jacob was Ngarrindjeri. He came from the Tatiara district in the south-east, near Bordertown, but as part of the government's policy of breaking up Aboriginal families he was sent as a boy to Poonindie in the west, just outside Port Lincoln on the Eyre Peninsula. Then he came to Adelaide, where he mastered the game of draughts and he became South Australia's champion draughts player. He toured Tasmania, and when he came back at one time he asked for Grandmother's hand in marriage. She was sixteen. He took her to Raukkan, and theirs was the last of the firestick marriages* to take place there. But there was no housing available on Raukkan, so they came back to Colley Reserve and camped there for several years longer. Grandmother had Mum and one or two of the other children there. Eventually they were given a house on Raukkan, so my grandmother left her mum and dad, and went to Raukkan and set up house.

Grandmother came to adopt Raukkan as her own home.

---

* A traditional marriage ceremony in which the families of the bride and groom formed processions carrying firesticks, which were symbolically placed together on the ceremonial site.

She got to know the language, got to know the people, and because Great-grandfather George Spender was Ngarrindjeri too, she got to know his people, and they got on very well. She was a well-respected lady down there. But Grandmother never forgot about being kicked off her land at Glanville.

Later Great-grandmother Lartelare and Great-grandfather George Spender went on to Raukkan as well. They'd just stay a few days, then they'd wander off to Hindmarsh Island or Goolwa. Eventually Great-grandfather George Spender died at Goolwa and was smoked on Mundoo Island, the island next to Hindmarsh Island.* Where he was buried, we don't know.

When she left the land at Glanville, Great-grandmother took up the name 'Mrs Glanville'. Wherever she went, she was always known as Mrs Glanville. She never lost the name from there. It meant something very dear to her, because Captain Hart and his wife were very kind to her. So the name 'Glanville' meant a lot to Grandmother, just as the place Glanville did. When they were kicked off, it broke her heart. She said to me, 'You won't be able to do anything about it while that factory stands. But the moment it's gone I want you to try and get that land back.'

The land at Glanville is very much a part of my heritage. In 1995, I made a claim for that land. You see, one day I was going along in the train from Adelaide, and I looked out the window and I saw them dismantling the factory that Grandma Glanville shook her fist at, because there had been a big fire. And I thought, wonderful! I can open my mouth now. I can start doing something about that land. My idea was to set up an elders' village there.

Now, there's a fellow that did want to buy this land and put eight houses on it, and when I told him of my idea for the land

---

* One of the funerary practices of Aboriginal people in South Australia involved drying the body by suspending it over a slow fire.

he said he was going to leave enough land to give back to me for an Aboriginal retirement village. But CSR didn't reply to him in relation to the sale of the land.

They can't touch the land within fifty metres either side of the Jervois Bridge. You can't build anything, which seems ridiculous, but it's because of the bridge. A car could come off, and that would be it for anyone living underneath! The only land they can touch now is the land where the CSR factory stood, and that's not available to us. The trouble is that now the ground is badly contaminated with arsenic, and to clean it up is going to cost a million dollars.

The Port Adelaide Council was all set to go with a redevelopment plan when I put in that claim for the Glanville site, and that stopped them from going any further with that land. There were Aboriginal students at the University of South Australia studying archaeology, and they wanted to do an archaeological dig on that site. The government has funded archaeological digs elsewhere, but they say they have no money, and the contamination on this particular site is a problem.

You know, when I first went to the State Minister of Aboriginal Affairs, who was Kim Mayes under the Labor government, one of his right-hand men challenged me and said, 'I go over the Jervois Bridge every morning to work, and there's no relevance of any Aboriginal history to me in that area.'

My reply was, 'How could there be? You're white.' So I was really worried about how this person was going to advise the minister. But fortunately I had a meeting with the State Heritage Committee, and they supported me fully on this issue. Now I've got more support, and my elders from the Ngarrindjeri side have also been able to furnish me with more information. They've been marvellous in helping me. At one stage a Lartelare Association was formed, and we were even looking at making a claim under the Native Title Act and the Land Acquisition Fund.

But recently there has been so much happening that I haven't had time to continue, and this claim has lapsed. I have to reconstitute a committee and get more information from CSR before I can go ahead with another claim. It's going to be a big fight, because that land's worth a lot of money. It's a big block. I believe my claim on that land was the only one on a site in South Australia that's in an inner-city suburb.

It's important to me as an Aboriginal person if I could get that land over there – not only for me but also for my community, so that my community can share it, black and white. I don't call my community just black. I call my community black and white, and it will be shared between black and white. Just as in the old days, when Grandmother lived there, and my great-grandmother, whatever work was here was shared between the black and the white. On the wharf, all the Aborigines that lived around there got work. There were good relationships, good reconciliation. It was greed that took all that away; and being Crown land, government land, if the government saw a chance to make money, no matter who was on it, off you went. That was what happened with Grandmother and her family.

I don't want a compensation payout for the land. I don't want money. I want the land, because I have plans for that land. If we can build an Aboriginal elders' retirement village there, it will not only benefit the elderly Aboriginal people, but also white people in the Port area, or from anywhere for that matter.

We were thinking of building an interpretive centre, but what the Port Adelaide Council thought would be nicer was to make a natural park. Well, I said, 'If you're going to put a natural park fifty metres either side of the bridge, you might as well put it all the way down to where the mangroves are.' So we're not sure what the final plans will be.

I'd like to see us do something like Camp Coorong, which is just out of Meningie. I often go there, because to me that is my spiritual rejuvenation place. I go back there when I need spiritual uplift, and I get it there because of all the learning that goes on there. They run cultural awareness camps, and they've got bush trails that you can walk on to learn all about the different food and medicines of that region. It was started by George and Tom Trevorrow, who work for the Ngarrindjeri Land and Progress Association, and Tom's wife Ellen teaches basket and mat weaving.

I hope we will be able to build up a similar operation here in Adelaide. We can have a walking trail along the Port River, and we can show people the different medicines that the Kaurna people used for healing and so on. It'll take a long time to get established, and I mightn't be around when it's finished, but hopefully the younger ones will take it on.

You know, in 1994 we had a Kaurna trail night when we followed a trail around the Port area and visited all the Kaurna sites. The then Liberal shadow minister joined us on the trail, but I didn't know it at the time. And after that trail we had an audience with him in Parliament House – Auntie Phoebe Wanganeen and I. You see, I believe if you can't get the ear of one party, you go to the other, so off we went to Parliament House. He was really interested, and I was pleased, because we need to get as many ideas and as much help as we can.

But I get tired sometimes, because I'm involved with so many other things, so it's good that all these different groups have been supporting me with my land at Glanville. I've got the Lartelare Association, the Kaurna Aboriginal Community Heritage Association, the Native Title group, the Port Adelaide environmental group, and we've got various council members from the Port Adelaide–Enfield Council, and we've got the Catholic Romero group, which is quite a big one. Then we've got individuals who are giving what help they can to get this native title business sorted out. But in this day and age, if you haven't got proof, with all the native title stuff and Mabo, it's very hard.

It's unreal when I see that Glanville site. I get certain feelings off that site from knowing that Lartelare has been walking around there. You feel it when you're Aboriginal – you can feel the spirits. But even as a white person I've been told you can feel those spirits. If you're genuine about it you'll feel the spirits there. Quite often I go down there and walk down by the Port River, and you can feel something's there. You know, I don't think I was ever meant to move out of the Port area, because I've tried living elsewhere, but I just had to come back to the Port to live.

Oh, I love to come down there and look at the pelicans that sit on the pylons in the river! They're gorgeous. I think they must know when I'm coming. I came down to the site recently and each pelican had its own pylon to perch on. I wonder why so many pelicans have come back like that? Maybe the old Aboriginal spirits are bringing them back, who knows?

Chapter 2

Childhood on Raukkan

I was born at Raukkan on 15 January 1941. My parents were Rebecca and Dan Wilson, and I came from a large family. I believe there were ten of us, but only five children survived. So I had three living brothers and one sister, as well as quite a few others who passed on when they were babies or toddlers. The ones that I remember living were my three older brothers, Bert, Doug and Graham – the oldest being Bert – and then there was my older sister Leila and myself. There was also Michael (Mikalo), but he was a foster-brother. He's still alive today and he lives with me, although he comes and goes from time to time. But that's how they came in order. Bert and Leila are gone. So that leaves Doug, Graham, Michael and myself.

My brothers and sisters cared for me a lot when I was little. I was the youngest one in the family, and I was born prematurely. I was only 2 pounds 12 ounces when I was born. In fact, I was so small my cot was a man's shoebox lined with cotton wool, and my mother used men's handkerchiefs for my nappies. They would keep me warm by putting my box on the oven door of the wood stove in the kitchen, and they had to keep that fire going day and night, even though it was summer time. I reckon that just shows that I was always going to be a survivor in life – no matter what barriers were placed before me.

Raukkan was formerly known as Point McLeay Mission, and before that it was known as Reid Town, but in later years they have reverted back to Raukkan, which was the original

Ngarrindjeri name for the area. Raukkan sits right on Lake Alexandrina. There was access by road, but a lot of people travelled by paddle-steamer to or from Goolwa. They would go directly across the lake and around Point Sturt, where you came to Goolwa, Hindmarsh Island, Mundoo Island and the Murray Mouth.

There were about three or four hundred people living on Raukkan then. The first houses built there were quite small, but in the 1940s they started building bigger places of up to four bedrooms. The Ngarrindjeri people were very good builders, and they made stone cottages and solid brick buildings. There was a school and a church. If you got sick, there was a nurse, a trained sister, in the little hospital, and the doctor used to visit from Tailem Bend.

My family used to live up a road called Top Row on the mission, going towards the cemetery and down to the old killing shed at Teringie. The Teringie flats ran down towards the lake. Walking up the Top Row from down the town, you had the school on your right, then our house. The first house on the left belonged to the Sumner family, the second house to the Rigney family, then the Rankines, then the Dodd family, and then Grandmother Glanville.

The houses changed residents from time to time. Living next to us at one stage were the Tripp family and the Heron family. I remember hearing my brothers talk of Auntie Sudie Heron – she had a beautiful voice, and often used to be described as the Aboriginal Nellie Melba. They wanted to take her away for training, but she said she wouldn't go.

The church at Raukkan is a dear little church, a lovely little church. I think of how the old seating was in the church, with the aisle down the middle and seats on both sides. The seating has changed now – it has long seats across the room with an aisle on each side of the church. That church used to be packed of a Sunday night for the meetings, and the singing was beautiful. You'd hear this beautiful harmonising. They had three services back then – morning service, then Sunday school, and then the night service. And the Christmas services in the church were packed, and the New Year services when we were seeing the old year out and the new year in.

There was one old fellow there who used to get the church ready for the night service, and he'd get down there and do his rounds. He was Mel Gollan, or Uncle Coonan, my mum's brother-in-law. He used to have to light those gas lamps that you had to pump. He'd be there pumping them up, and then he would place the great big speakers outside the church, and he'd play records or tapes of hymns sung by various artists – Pat Boone and others. The people would be lying around on their front lawns or verandahs listening to the music. On a summer evening you'd hear the hymns all over Raukkan. And that old fellow looked after the church. It was always clean, and it had fresh flowers – the ladies always took in fresh flowers for Sunday church. And the lights were kept spotless. He made sure that everything was looked after and polished, and so did the ladies.

The Salvation Army ministers used to preach in my day there. Once they used to have local Nunga preachers on Raukkan – the older ones, like Mark Wilson, Harold Kropinyeri and David Unaipon – and I believe they were quite good, but that was before my time. They were called lay preachers. It was mainly the Army that preached there when I was young. Originally the mission was Congregational, but then they went to Salvation Army, and had a turn of Army preachers come and go from Adelaide over to Raukkan. Each one of them would stay for a time and do their work there. They'd set up social programs for the women and the children, and they'd take the Sunday services. It was good. Some of the Army officers they had visiting would come out and play in the bands and timbral brigades.

It's always good to go home and go to that little church. That little old church holds lots of memories – all the people who have passed on who were taken there to say goodbye to, people who you've seen get married there, and others who worked in the church. But these days, we seem to be visiting it quite frequently, with all these funerals. We've lost a lot of our people over the last few years.

Just only recently we were on Raukkan at a funeral, and some of us were sitting there in the church looking around. And one old girl said, 'I can remember every Sunday coming down from the Top Row.' It was Blanche Jackson – BJ, we used to call her. She continued, 'My hair was all done up with those ribbons. My mother had them perfect. But when I'd get there, I'd pull all those ribbons out. I hated them!' And then we started talking about how we'd spend each harvest thanks-giving in the church. They had a platform at the front, and we'd be all standing up there with our Sunday best on, all dressed up. And we'd be singing these little children's songs – 'Hear the pennies dropping, listen as they fall'. You can never bring those days back; they're gone for ever. But the memories of them are still there.

*

No one was rich in those days, but the very little income that our parents got kept the home going. You didn't have electricity, you didn't have gas, but you didn't pay rent either. We had a good time with our parents. It was the white bosses and overseers that came in and made things hard for us – well, for our parents. But back in those days, as kids growing up, we didn't know what was going on with the Aborigines Protection Board.

Mother was a domestic on Raukkan, where she got work if they had the jobs there to give. If not, she was just home most of the time, but I remember when I was little going out to Glenora, the dairy farm, and watching her milk the cows. She had to do the milking by hand and then separate the cream. She worked there for maybe twelve months – six to twelve months on and off. I remember the dairy, and walking home about half a kilometre with her. Her right leg had a nasty ulcer on it. I think it was from a knock or scratch she got once working in the vineyards. It never healed, so for years and years she struggled with that leg.

My father Dan worked in the government store for over thirty years. In those days all his hard work was never recognised. I think by the time he died he had worked something like thirty-five or thirty-seven years in the store. Then the day he finished, or two days after he finished, he developed a bad heart.

Dad's father, my grandfather, Dan Wilson, used to have a wurlie down by the lake, and he used to do transcendental travelling. He used to tell Great-grandmother, 'When I'm in that trance in my wurlie, don't let nobody touch me, or you'll disturb my travel.' So she'd sit outside and keep watch while he'd travel and go and see his people. A couple of hours later, he'd wake up and tell them how everyone was, and bring messages from them. The younger people didn't do that. They stopped because of colonisation. Even practising their own culture was seen as evil, and they would have been called witches and warlocks if it were known they were doing something like that. I was told about this by an elder from Raukkan, my aunt Dorothy Sumner, Mutha Doog, my dad's cousin.

*

I have many fond memories of growing up on Raukkan. My fondest memories are of my younger years when I was always playing with my mates, or going to different social functions with the family. They used to have dances or concerts, and we'd all go along to the shows. These shows were held without any alcohol around, as this was a part of the Aborigines Protection Board ruling: NO ALCOHOL – but that didn't stop the ones drinking it from getting it in. We'd have a good time, because our parents would be taking part, particularly my mum and my sister. It was great to see them up there on the stage, acting out. People would do skits and put on shadow plays – pretending to operate on people, pulling strings of sausages out of their stomachs and so on. And when you look back on those years, you only wish that those people were still around.

Friday night always used to be a treat night for us. They used to have pictures on in the local hall. You'd pay your ten cents, or a shilling as it was in those days – that was a lot of money back then – and we'd also get twopence from Dad to spend in the canteen on lollies. We'd get quite a lot for twopence. I always used to buy the liquorice blocks – they called them nigger blocks. You'd get four blocks per penny. You felt pretty good when you had all these blocks in your little bag. If you were lucky enough to be able to buy chocolate, you were rich! Then, after buying your lollies, you went into the hall and sat down and watched the pictures. My favourites were the pictures about pirates.

Friday night was also a treat night at home. My dad was a real good cook. While we were out playing in the afternoon, or at school, Dad would be home cooking. Come the end of the pictures that night, we'd all go home, and there were pasties and cakes and all sorts of goodies – you name it, he cooked it. We'd all have a good feed, and then my brothers would sit up and play draughts. I'd watch them for a little while, and then I'd be told to get to bed. I'd had a good time, so off I'd go to bed and leave all the rest watching this famous draughts game – making all the noise, telling who to move and where to move.

There were never any rich families on Raukkan. The money-makers were the gun shearers who used to go out to the sheep properties. They used to have plenty of money, but they had to work very hard. In those days, when we were under the control of the Aborigines Protection Board, the wage that you earned on the mission was just enough to keep you going from week to week, even though you could buy a lot more for your money.

I always used to get second-hand shoes, but I soon learnt not to grumble or grizzle about it. And at Christmas time, it was always just the basic toys – never the real costly toys or dolls. One year I got a rag doll, and I cried and cried because the girl over the road got one of those nice celluloid dolls. Did I get a hiding! And the rag doll got taken away as well.

We were a family. We never ever went without. Dad always made sure that we had food and the basics. I remember my older brothers coming home with big wheat bags full of fish. They'd go fishing – my dad used to go down with them – and fill up these wheat bags with callop about a foot long and bigger. They'd get callop and perch from Lake Alexandrina. You'd see them, bag after bag come in. They'd chuck them in the trough, and fish would be jumping everywhere. They'd be scaling them, cutting them up, and you'd know that there would be another big feast that night. If other people didn't have anything to eat, they would take the fish and share it with them.

My father also used to go to Hindmarsh Island and down around the lake swan egging, and he'd come home and the boat would be nearly full of swan eggs. One swan egg would be equivalent to three chooks' eggs. They're lovely for cooking. My father would pack up some eggs and take them down to families who needed food and make sure they had whatever they needed. We always had that sharing attitude when we were growing up – sharing things, this is where my attitude today has come from, I guess, part of my nature for sharing with others – giving whenever I can, or helping and nursing whenever people are sick.

One time I had a bad chest, and the cold wouldn't leave me, and I ended up staying in bed for seven months. I was very weak, and Mum used to get pretty tired looking after me. She was working at the dairy then, milking the cows. So different ones used to come in and sit with me, and look after me until Mum got home. They didn't look for any payment – they'd just do it because they knew that Mum had to work. But then Mum would always give them a bit of food or whatever in return.

You know, I want to take my grandkids down to Raukkan for a weekend, to let them see what life was like without videos and TV. Although it's all spoilt now, Raukkan – they've got TV there and electricity. But if these kids were to go down to Raukkan when there wasn't any electricity there, and just see how we used to live, like with the old wood stove . . .

Like my father said, 'You know, you got to learn to accept what you haven't got. Because when you haven't got it, you won't look for it.' And I've always remembered that, even today. And now I can live my life with the bare essentials. I don't need a lot to keep me going. Whereas lots of other people I know are very materialistic, unfortunately. I think some of them go through terrible anguish because they haven't got the material things that they want. If I haven't got a penny in my purse, then that's no worries. I know it's nothing compared to the things we didn't have years ago. I'm more interested in my heritage and spirituality and genealogy. And I like looking at the cultural side of life, and relating to my culture, which I love.

*

I had lots of mates around me growing up on Raukkan. Play on the mission meant making our own fun. There was a big pepper tree at the house opposite us on the Top Row, and if Tarzan was ever around in those days it was in that back yard! We tied so many ropes on the limbs, and we'd swing from branch to branch. We had a great time.

We also used to build cubby houses and dig trenches all over Raukkan to play in. Sometimes we didn't fill the trenches in and the older people would fall in them, and then there'd be trouble!

One year in summer, fires were burning in the Adelaide Hills, and the smoke came right across the lake from the very early morning, right throughout the day. Huge billows of smoke came across and dropped ash in the lake. Then a storm developed and the waves built up on the lake, which brought in all these turtles. They brought little ones with them – little *thukabis*. So we chased the turtles up and down the beach. Their babies came with them, so we started catching them. When the storm and the wind subsided, and the smoke had gone, we put the turtles back in the water and let them swim away. It was a lovely sight to see these big turtles – I'd never seen them before.

They had a Back To Raukkan gathering there a few years ago, and it was good to see some of my old mates come back, and to remember with them some of those things we got up to. And did we have a good laugh! As you get older you yearn to be able to sit down with your old mates and talk about those days. And once you've talked about them you seem to get some sense of relief, because a lot of us have had such very hard lives, so it helps to remember the good times we had.

I've had a lot of people my age and older come to me in recent years and say, 'Look, I sit down and I think about the past all the time, and I cry. And I play my hymns, and I cry. Is that silly?' But I tell them, 'No, that's not silly, because you're only expressing what you feel.' Because many of the old people are living on their own now. They've got no one to talk to, so they express their sadness in their tears. There's nothing wrong with that. I do that myself sometimes. I think it's because we are missing those who are gone too. I sit down and sometimes I cry for Leila, who has now passed away, because Leila was my only sister. I think to myself, it's so lonely here without her. She was always there when I needed her. And even though I wasn't young when she died, when she did leave us, I really felt that Leila not being there for me any more had put a big hole in my life.

Leila at an early age.

Chapter 3

Holidays Down on the Coorong

When I was a kid we'd never miss spending Christmas holidays down on the Coorong, or Kurrangk as it is also called, and how I like to call it. The Coorong is a ninety-mile stretch of water running south from the Murray Mouth, between the coast and the sandhills of the Younghusband Peninsula. We went there every year until I was about twelve. In those days there were eight weeks holiday over the summer, so we'd pack up all our supplies and head down to a place called Ngarlung, on the sea side of the Coorong, just opposite Pelican Point. Dad's people came from that side of the Coorong, and we'd go to the same place year in and year out.

Each family had their certain spots along the Coorong, their own cultural lands. There were the Dodds and the Sumners and the Rankines who had Marks Point, the Lovegroves who had Pelican Point, then you had us, the Wilsons, who had Ngarlung. Going along the Coorong you had these different camps, all these people identifying with their cultural lands. If anyone came down, we'd always welcome them in, or they would welcome us or any others going to their campsites. Different families would spend evenings together, talking and sharing food. The old people would speak Ngarrindjeri together as they sat around the campfire at night, particularly when we were camping down at Ngarlung.

It was real fun for us, just roaming in the sandhills and swimming in the Coorong – that was our fun times. It was the best time we ever had, those eight weeks of the year. And each year it didn't change; it was always the same.

Someone from Raukkan would take us down to Pelican Point on the old horse-trolley. It would take us about half a day to get there. Meanwhile, my father would load up the boat, the *Gayvon*, and row it around from Raukkan. He'd come to the barrage that separates the Coorong from Lake Alexandrina, go through the locks, and then pull around to Pelican Point with the boat. Then we'd spend two days with the Lovegroves at Pelican Point getting ready to take everything over to Ngarlung, on the other side. In those two days, Dad would go across from Pelican Point to Ngarlung and clean up a camping spot. He'd make sure that an area was cleaned and all ready for the boat to go over with our supplies. In the meantime the boys would have a windbreak made, all the sticks ready for the wurlies and the hessian bags all sewn together, and when Dad was ready, over we'd go.

All the blankets and food got taken over, then the camp would be set up. Dad and my brothers would build the wurlies out of sticks and sewn bags. It took quite a few trips to get everyone across – maybe two to carry our things, and three more to get all of us across the Coorong. There would be our family, Grandmother, two cousins and about four extras, so you would be looking at nearly twenty people.

I remember there was this old fella who used to live there, old Hubert Tripp – we used to call him Uncle. Uncle Hubert always lived at Ngarlung; he'd built a hut there. He was an old ex-serviceman, and had a war service pension. He'd live off the land down there, and occasionally he'd row the boat all the way up to Goolwa to get supplies. Somehow he always seemed to know exactly when we were coming to Ngarlung each year. He'd row up to Goolwa and he'd buy a big bag of boiled lollies. He'd spend the night up there, then he'd come back the next day. We'd see him coming in the morning, rowing the boat. And he'd be there to welcome us to Ngarlung with this big bag of sweets – maybe one or two for each of us. That was a special treat for us from Uncle Hubert. Afterwards, he came down some days to the camp and had a meal with us and did things for us.

Apart from that, lollies were unheard of there. We lived off whatever we got. There wasn't any alcohol, and people didn't look for it. You could kill whatever you wanted for your food, because it wasn't a national park then.

We learnt how to find water. My dad knew where to look, and he taught us how to look for it. I used to see him clear away the sand and dig down, and you could swear there was a little fridge underneath the ground that gave up all this clear, icy-cold water. Not a drop of sand was in the water we drank. And we had plenty of fish to eat. I had a brother who was nearly seven foot tall, and I've seen him carry fish bigger than him that came out of the Coorong. Yum, mulloway!

And damper – we had fresh damper every meal. You didn't know what fresh bread was like until you got back to Raukkan. Damper was a lot better. We used to have damper with butter, Vegemite and jam all at once. We thought it was lovely. Sometimes we had to make really big dampers. Of course, we had to feed a whole camp, and every day was a busy day down there. We would be going out chopping wood, preparing it for the fires, and making sure all the buckets were filled with water. Dad would make the buckets from kerosene tins and put wire handles on, and we had to make sure that they were filled with plenty of water for whenever it was needed.

We used to eat rabbits, and we also had *nganingi* – white-fellas call them pigfaces. And we ate *kalathami* – little white berries that used to grow on a tree. They're real juicy. Also cockles. We'd eat swan eggs, which Dad would get from Hindmarsh Island. We had no kangaroo or wallabies, but we did eat swan, *kungari*, and Cape Barren geese, *lawarri*. Swan is quite lovely when it's cooked properly, and the Cape Barren geese are better still. The swan meat is dark red, but Cape Barren is just like an ordinary roast duck. We used to roast them in the wood stove at Raukkan, but down the Coorong we'd cook them in the big camp oven.

My mum and grandmother were always sewing bags together for our wurlies. Sometimes the wind would blow a bit too harsh; it used to break the bags or tear them. So we were always sewing bags. We had a pile of bags there, or old blankets, all ready to put around the wurlies. We really needed them on the sea side of the Coorong, because of the strong wind that blew in there.

My grandmother – that's Grandmother Glanville – would sit and weave things. She'd sit down there at Ngarlung and make mats and baskets. First she'd have to pull these special flat reeds to get them ready for weaving, and then she'd sit down and start making something.

When we were at Ngarlung we'd be miles away from the doctor or the hospital, and if we needed anything we had to go to Goolwa by boat, or go back to Raukkan. One year I dived off the pylons that they used to hold the fishing nets, and instead of diving out into the deeper water, I dived in towards the shore, into the shallow water, and I tore all my stomach and my leg on the coral. There was blood everywhere, and a mad panic as the other swimmers ran down to get Dad. He had a little bit of iodine that he poured all over my cuts. Then he went into the bush and went walking around looking for this special bush medicine. Before long he comes back with some stuff – I don't know what it was, but he beat it up into a paste, and then he plastered it all on me. Mum was worried, and she said, 'Is she going to be all right?' Dad said, 'She'll be all right.' And you know, I never needed a doctor. My cuts all soon healed, and even the scar went away. So whatever he found and used, it was pretty good bush medicine.

There were a lot of bush medicines that the old Ngarrindjeri people used to use to help heal themselves. They used the bush medicines right up until the medical clinic got set up on Raukkan, and then they stopped using them. I've seen them use Old Man's Beard, that white stuff you see growing on the bushes down the Coorong. You mix it up and use it as a poultice to put on your joints or on your sores. And they used to drink the juice. I don't mind using the poultice on my joints, but I don't know about drinking it. Don't know what's going down inside!

There was another thing that we got up to as kids down the Coorong – Leila and I used to laugh about this. Near our camp there used to be a fishermen's hut, just like one tin room, almost at the end of the Hummocks, near the Murray Mouth. In that hut the fishermen used to keep biscuits – tins and tins of biscuits. But, you see, there was also this old horse there. I don't know where he came from – maybe he got over that side of the Coorong with the fishermen.

This particular day the adults had told us to get out and go and play. So off we went, and we found this hut – *and* all these milk arrowroot biscuits! We grabbed them – we went mad. After we'd had a good feed, Leila came out of the hut, and she still had a biscuit in her mouth. But the old horse came out from the side of the shack at the same time, and she came face to face with it, and it bit her biscuit clean off! We screamed and ran back to the camp, but in our panic we'd forgotten we still had handfuls of biscuits. And did we get a hiding when we got back! The old people knew they were the fishermen's biscuits. We had to take 'em back and put 'em all back in the hut. And we were told not to go near the old hut again.

We also had a little ducky-boat about a quarter the size of a dinghy, and that little boat was left there for us to play around on, just on the shore. We'd collect the jellyfish – picking 'em up and putting them on the boat – and we'd pile them all up and watch them melt in the sun and run away to nothing.

I wasn't allowed to get in the bigger dinghy, or if I did I was to stay just at the shore. But one day I put the paddles in and I rowed out to the middle of the Coorong. It was only then that I realised how far out I was. And they were all yelling out to me from the shore, telling me to sit down in the boat. But instead I decided, in my panic, to jump overboard into the channel. It was lucky I had my brother Graham's polo-neck jumper on, because the water went under and puffed it up like a float, and that's what kept me up.

There was this fella, old Albert Mack, coming up behind me in a boat, and they were all yelling and waving their arms on the shore to tell me he was there. But I couldn't hear what they were saying to me. In the end my brother Graham had to swim out and get me, but by the time he had got to shore with me, the boat had drifted all the way over to the barrage, so then he had to swim across to the barrage and get the boat and bring it back. And did I get a hiding for that, because I could've drowned and also I could've lost the boat. So that was a hard lesson I had to learn.

While we were at Ngarlung, Dad would take us across the sand dunes to the ocean beach on the other side. We'd all march over there in line, because there were snakes on the dunes. Dad had very sharp eyes. He'd lead us all across the dunes along the Coorong, and he'd say, 'Now, watch where I walk. Follow my steps so you won't get into trouble.'

On the way to the ocean we'd collect *manthirri*, berries of a shrub on the sand dunes. We'd each have a can, and we'd get buckets full. Once we'd crossed the dunes, we'd get down to the ocean, the Great Southern Ocean, and it was beautiful. We'd collect the cockles in bags from the ocean, take them back to the camp, then we'd make a big fire and chuck them on, and they'd open up when they were cooked. After gathering cockles we'd run along the beach, looking to see what else we could find. We'd get big glass balls that were used as floats for the fishing nets, and we'd also find fluorescent lights and captains' hats, and all sorts of different things. All kinds of boats and ships were wrecked along there, and all these things would come right up on to the shore.

Once Graham, my brother, found a hand-grenade. He carried it all the way home, and it wasn't until we got home that we realised it was still live. So Dad had to row across to Pelican Point and go up to the big house there, to get them to ring Goolwa. They sent the military down, and they came and detonated it.

At Ngarlung we'd watch the fishing boats when they'd come into the Coorong from Goolwa. They had to turn the boats on their sides to get them through, because the water was so shallow. And I can remember, I think it was when Queen Mary died, we were all down there at Ngarlung, and all the boats were going up and down the Coorong with their flags at half mast.

One year down there, we'd been over to Pelican Point, yarning with the Lovegroves on the other side and having a nice time. Before we went home, Dad sent my brother and my cousin Bulla across in the boat to check our camp. They had to lift all the mattresses and check there wasn't anything underneath, because it was hot weather and there were snakes around. They went over and came back and said everything was clear. So, thinking that they'd checked everything, off we all went, back to Ngarlung.

When we got home, Mum said to me, 'Come on, get to bed.'

And I said, 'No, I can't! I can't lay down there.' When I tried to lie down, there was something under the mattress. I could feel it.

'Go on, lay down!' Mum said.

'No, I can't, I don't want to lay down here.'

'No, you lay down!' But no, I couldn't. So I'd get up again.

My Uncle Proctor was living with us then, and he had crutches because he only had one leg. So he got his crutches and flipped the blankets off and lifted the mattress up, and underneath there was this big snake. The boys hadn't gone back to check the camp at all. They just went to the middle of the Coorong, then rowed back again. They killed that snake and then they threw it into the Coorong.

Uncle Hubert Tripp continued to stay at Ngarlung until he got very, very sick and he had to leave. The fishermen bought him out. They bought his hut and everything, and now they've got a lease on Ngarlung for their fishing. They've even got electricity generators there.

One time, there was another old fella who came to the Coorong to live – Old Amos. He used to make things out of skin – snakeskin and lizard skin. He'd make pouches or wallets and things like that. He was another nice old gentleman, and he got to know all my family. He ended up living there for a long time.

So these men who used to live there found solace, I guess, in living out there all alone in that country, in the wilderness. And they had a great time, and they never did want to leave there. I can understand that, because Ngarlung really was a beautiful place. Each year that's what we looked forward to – going to that place. It was like a second home.

We'd come back a week before school started again. We felt privileged when we got back to the mission, because we were able to go away for the holidays – just being with the family for the whole eight weeks, and enjoying each other's company in that really lovely place. And I guess that's why Leila wrote her lovely poem called 'The Coorong: Land of my Father's People':

My sister was a very wise and wonderful person – in her

own way she was a bit of a historian. She loved the Coorong, or the Kurrangk as it's called, and her ashes were taken back there when she died, to be scattered on a point where she most loved to sit. She'd look out towards Hindmarsh Island and across the lake to the big hill on Raukkan, and down towards Noonameena, so she had an all-round view. And at the foot of her was the most beautiful old Ngarrindjeri burial ground. She always wanted to go back there one day – that was her wish. So we took her back – we took her ashes back.

The Coorong

Land of my father's people,
place of my ancestors' past,
never will I forget you,
for you are dear to my heart.

I've climbed your golden sand-dunes,
and walked through your native scrub,
swum in your sea-green waters,
watched the birds, in their evening flight.

Oh how my heart is longing
to hear the song of the surf
from the mighty Southern Ocean
whose shores I often trod.

The many lovely wild flowers
whose seeds are scattered by the winds
like a cloak of many colours
grow there, within your folds.

The midden heaps around me,
the bleached bones on the shore
are fragments of a lifetime
which I yearn to know once more.

Through the wind and sand around me
at night by the camp fire bright,
midst the blue smoke wafting upwards,
I recall my ancestors' life.

Oh spirit of the long ago
and guardian of the past
as I stand beside your waters,
my soul knows peace at last.

Leila D. Rankine

Chapter 4

Friends and Elders

Growing up on Raukkan was when I made all my friends. We grew up together, and then, going through school together on Raukkan, we got even closer.

Before I went to school, my mother often came away to Adelaide. She'd go down to McLaren Vale, where they used to pick grapes, and I'd come with her. My brothers and my sister were older than me and were all in school. One time, just before I started school, I remember going down the vineyards to play with some other kids. We loved throwing dirt at each other. It was a game, you see; you hid behind the vines and you threw all the dark dirt from in the vineyards – but we didn't know what was in it.

One particular day, oh boy, did my eyes get a load of dirt in them! Then the next morning I woke up and my face was all swollen. My eyes were sore and puffy, and I could barely open them – only maybe just a squint. I was trying to see out of them to see where I was going. My mother rushed me into the Children's Hospital, and they kept me in there because I had a very bad eye infection caused through that dirt.

As the days got on I went blind, and so they had to operate. I was blind for three months, and for all that time I never left that hospital. But there was an Aboriginal woman working there at that time, and I used to call her 'my eyes'. She used to come and get me and take me outside – she'd lead me and take me out for walks. I knew it was sunny, because I could feel the sunshine on me, and I knew when it was cold because she'd put a warm jacket on me, and I could feel the wind blowing on my face. I loved her; her name was Elsie Summerfield – a beautiful person.

For three months I didn't see anything. When they took the bandages off I could see, but it was a bit blurry. It finally cleared, but it left me with a left eye problem – it's a lazy eye and it will only move when it wants to, or it'll move in a different direction to the other. So this meant that I had to have glasses. Coming home from Adelaide to a place like Raukkan with these tiny little glasses on, I thought it was terrible! Then having to start school with them – that just wasn't on. Wherever I went, the kids used to call me 'four-eyes' and 'glassy eyes', and all the other names that kids get called.

So I didn't want to go to school because of these glasses. I did absolutely everything in my power to make sure I could never find them in the mornings. I'd hide them, and I tried all sorts of tricks. Then one day I broke them – on purpose – and did I get a hiding for it! But I still wouldn't wear them. Anyway, Mum couldn't afford any more, so I had to go without.

One day there were four of us playing tennis – Arthur Milera, Rufus Rigney, Pam Dodd and myself were playing doubles. I got in close to the net, and as I came up, Rufus hit the ball down towards the other end, but the ball hit me straight in the eye – the same eye that I had damaged before. So I was blind again for another month or more. Then they thought that eye had burst inside, so again they had to get me down to Adelaide to look at it. But it was OK. Rufus, who hit the ball, never ever forgot that incident. Rufus and Arthur have since passed on.

We had a liking for sport at Raukkan – we had football, basketball and tennis. I also loved softball, and cricket too. During one of the games I played, as a left-hand batter, I caught Rufus back with the bat. I swung it back and laid him out cold. Poor old Rufus. I reckon he never looked to play cricket again, especially with me!

We had a girls' basketball team, and it was a good one too. We played against other schools in the district, like Meningie or Murray Bridge, Tailem Bend, Narrung. And we had a good vigoro team. We always travelled out to play against other teams, because I think, with the mission being under the Protection Board, they weren't allowed to come in to play us at the mission. We used to travel to our matches by bus up to the townships. I know we won matches, and I think we did win a premiership or two.

And swimming too. One of the fun things about growing up on Raukkan was the swimming times. We had some really good swimmers; being born by a lake did help. Lake Alexandrina is a beautiful lake.

On the hill on Raukkan that overlooks the jetty and the lake is a monument in memory of Captain Charles Sturt, and the day he landed there after travelling down the Murray. From the town up to the monument and down to the lake it was about a five-minute walk – two minutes if it was stinking hot and you wanted to get there in a hurry! We couldn't wait to get out of school to go swimming on hot days. We ran like hell.

On the weekends, we'd go down to the lake in the morning and swim until we just about dropped – just before the sun went down in the evening. And we'd do all sorts of things once we got down to that jetty. We'd play cricket on the jetty; we would hit the ball into the water and someone would dive for it. You'd soon come back up with it, and sometimes you'd not only have the boys chasing after it but you could have a snake or two following it as well. So you had to be very careful and very quick.

I wasn't much of a swimmer, but if I had to I could save my life in the water. I wouldn't have gone under, although it nearly happened a couple of times. If you couldn't swim very well, you'd follow the posts out one by one till you got to the end of the jetty, and then you could say you'd achieved something. To reach the end of the jetty was a famous thing to do at Raukkan. You got a few pats on the back if you made it to the end.

Growing up on Raukkan, you did things you were allowed to, and you did things you weren't allowed to. And swimming away from the jetty was one of the things we weren't allowed to do. That was an important thing I had to learn, because if you swam away from the jetty, it meant that you swam away from the safe area in the lake. There were spots where there were currents, and the old people knew that it was dangerous to swim there.

But we didn't listen. Three or four of us girls decided to swim across from the distant shore to the end of the jetty, instead of swimming along the jetty and following it post by post. We got halfway, and then we started to hit a rip. And it was scrambles and pulling on each other and screaming. But we got out, and we soon realised that we daren't tell anybody, because we knew what we had done. But unfortunately somebody saw us, and they reported us, and we all got a hiding for it. I suppose it was for the best, because we could've drowned and no one would've seen us.

I had some good friends on Raukkan, and I didn't fight with any of them. My girlfriend over the road, Pam, who I grew up with all those years, was a good mate. But my dearest friend was Gloria, Gloria Sparrow, or Gloria Rigney then. We had many fun times together. Gloria used to love parading on the jetty in her red bikini. We also pinched fruit off the trees together in the orchard. You were never allowed to do that. The old ones would soon tell you off. One night we were up there at the orchard, pinching fruit, and one of the old ones caught us. It was Gloria's dad, but he came and helped himself too, and he kept our fruit as well, didn't he! So who was the thief, and who wasn't? We walked into his house the next day and saw the fruit sitting on their table, and they were having a good feed of it. But I guess the old ones were showing us that they didn't want anything to happen to us while we were living on the mission.

It made you start to listen a bit more – it was part of growing up and learning discipline. Like with funerals on Raukkan. Now, with children today, you'll see them standing anywhere and everywhere, looking at funeral processions as they go past. As kids we were never allowed to do that. Our grandfathers and grandmothers told us, 'You're not to watch the funeral', and they'd close up the curtains and go out. We had to be inside with the blinds pulled across, and that was it! You waited inside until the funeral procession had passed your house, and if you opened the windows, or if you were seen by your parents peeping through, you were in trouble. You didn't get chastised then – it was all left until everything was over. They'd just walk in casually after the funeral, and *crack!* you really copped it.

You were never allowed to speak of the ones who'd passed on, and all their things would be put away. Then, after twelve months, their photos would be brought out again and you'd talk about the person and have a few laughs at the funny things they'd done. It was like a welcoming back for the person who'd died.

Then things started to change about the time I went to high school, and we were allowed to go to funerals. With the change in government policies, the old people must have thought, well, they're changing things, so now we have to change.

I had lots of uncles and aunties, and I had lots of carers – people who watched over you and took an interest in you as you grew up on Raukkan. Being cared for by others when you were very young, you had more than enough people around you. When you were older, you were told to get outside and play. But if you were inside, one thing you weren't allowed to do was butt in. If you were inside, if your mother and father were talking to anyone, you had to sit there quiet. They would crack you if they thought you were being cheeky. We weren't even allowed to talk at the table. If you talked, your meal would be taken away from you. So you had to learn to sit there, be quiet and use your manners.

It was all a lesson in discipline; you do what you're told and you listen or you get a hiding. Learning that part of the culture was good, and I appreciate that today – that discipline I got then. I still try to discipline the younger ones today – the grandchildren – as they're growing up. Otherwise you miss some of these old ways, like being respectful to our elders.

As kids we loved to sit down and chat with the old people, but you had to be very careful how you spoke to them and take care with the questions that you asked. Because if you asked something that you shouldn't have, you were in big trouble, and you soon knew about it.

I remember there was one old lady on Raukkan when I was about four years old. Mutha Toke was her name, and she used to go and see my grandmother – that's Grandmother Glanville. I had this little spade and I used to go up the back of the houses opposite us and play along the top of the rise there. This time, I'm digging away and all of a sudden I see Mutha Tokie coming, and I'm thinking to myself, I'll have a yarn to her. The man who kills sheep for the mission is coming down the road behind her, so as she gets close, I say to her, 'Oh, Mutha Tokie, butcher's coming down there.'

She said, 'What, my girl?' with her pipe still in her mouth – she always smoked a pipe. So I repeated, 'Butcher coming.' But then she started to get angry, and I thought to myself, goodness me, what have I done now? What have I said? So I tried to explain again, 'There's a butcher coming over there behind you.' She got really angry then, and she started to come at me with her walking stick. That was enough for me. I got up quick smart and ran for home. It didn't take me long to get home, me being younger and a lot faster than her.

When I got in the door, I shut it real quick, and my mother said to me suspiciously, 'What's wrong?'

'Oh, nothin',' I said.

But next thing – bang, bang, bang on the door. It was Mutha Tokie there with her walking stick.

My father was there, and he opened the door and asked, 'What's the matter, Mutha Tokie?'

'That girl in there?' she said. 'The way she talked to me! She's naughty. She's been telling me Butcher coming!'

Well, did I get a hiding! When all the tears had subsided and were gotten over with – as well as the hiding – I asked my parents, 'Why did I get a hiding?'

And Mum explained, 'Well, her husband's name is Butcher, and you saying it to her got her upset. He's been dead for some time.'

You know, I learnt the hard way. They didn't tell you these things. I had to get to know the elders and who they were, and how to respect them. She was a dear old girl, that old lady Mutha Tokie, and I grew up then to respect her. I had to go and apologise to her, which I did.

'Little girl,' she said, 'That's all right, my girl. You know now. You won't say that to Mutha Tokie no more.'

And I said, 'No, Mutha.'

Another thing I had to learn was never to call my elders by their first names. They became Uncle or Auntie so-and-so. 'Mutha' is a form of 'grandmother', and when they're old like that it's better to call them Mutha than Auntie.

The kind of discipline that we had in those days was very firm, but I never regret from that day to this the discipline that

I got, because it made us respect our elders. They didn't thrash us out of the ordinary; you got your smack and that was it. And they didn't go back and reiterate over what had happened. They told you once, and that was it. And their form of discipline came from anyone. Your elders were allowed to tell you off any time and anywhere they saw fit. If you weren't doing the right thing, you were grabbed by the ear and hauled home, and then you'd be given another hiding when you got home! So growing up on Raukkan had its good days and its bad days.

*

When I was growing up, I had many silent thoughts about my mother's marital problems. I think at one stage there my mother and father separated. Later it became apparent to me that my mother had fallen in love with another chap, Proctor Wilson, my dad's cousin. She left my dad and took myself and my brother and sister down to McLaren Vale, where she lived with him. My older brother stayed at Raukkan.

Years later I received a letter from Mrs Marjorie Angas, previously a welfare officer of the Aborigines Protection Board, telling me about this great love affair between my mother and Proctor Wilson. The letter said that my mum was ordered back to Raukkan by the Protection Board and told to go back to her husband. You see, they had a hold on her, because if she didn't go back, then they could have taken us children away.

There was always this constant threat over people with children. The happiness of the children didn't count. The Protection Board just laid this on us, and that was it. We had to jump when told, or else! That was their way of dealing with you.

Mum moved back to Raukkan, but in her letter Mrs Angas said it was the saddest love story that you ever heard. She said if my mother had stayed with Proctor maybe life would have been a lot better for her, as Mum didn't deserve the cruel treatment she received.

On numerous occasions I came to live with aunts in the city, and I guess that was my mother's way of protecting me from the situation. When I look further back into my life I realise there may have been domestic violence in my home, and so to protect me from seeing it, I guess, my mum brought me to live with my aunties. But I didn't see any of it. It was my brothers who saw it.

My older brother Graham saw it – he saw quite a bit. At times gone past, when he used to drink, Graham became quite angry when he spoke about that part of our family life. But for a long time I couldn't work out what he was angry about. I couldn't fit the puzzle together, until one day it all clicked. What Graham was talking about was himself seeing Mum in this situation, being bashed by Dan, who at times could be cruel.

On one occasion Mum grabbed a full tin of jam off the top of the cupboard, and she hit Dan over the head with it, and it knocked him out. She thought she'd killed him, so she took off up to Grandmother's place – Laura Glanville, my grandmother, who lived just up the road a bit – and she stayed there until she knew that things were all right to go home. She knew that when we kids were out of school, we'd walk home, so she'd go home then. But we never saw any of this. My brother was the only one that saw it, and he never said anything about it – only when he was drinking did talk of this violence come out.

I thought Dan was my father. Sometimes I heard people talking, and I used to ask Leila, after Mum was gone. But she wouldn't tell me. You could only say certain things, you know. Eventually, about eighteen years ago, I said to Leila, 'Come on now. Heavens above, can't you tell me? I'm old enough to know now.'

So she said, 'All right, sit down.' And so she told me. Dan wasn't my father at all; it was Proctor – Proctor Wilson.

I said, 'Well, why didn't anyone tell me when my father was still alive?'

You see, my father, Proctor Wilson, was a lovely person – a very gentle person. And he loved us. He died in Glenside Hospital from war injuries and pneumonia. He'd been shell-shocked, and he was affected by nerve gas. He'd also had his leg blown off in France. So Proctor eventually went to Glenside mental hospital, and he died there.

But I only knew Dan as my father, up until I was told otherwise by Leila. When I was born, Dan was there. He was the only one I ever knew as my father. But Proctor was actually the father of both Graham and myself. All the rest were Dan's children. But we didn't see each other as being different. We were all brothers and sisters.

Michael Rigney is another brother of mine. He was fostered to us by my cousin, Patricia Gollan. She had him before she was married, and when she was getting married she didn't want Michael growing up with someone he didn't know as his dad. Pat felt that Mum and Dad would make good parents for Michael, so Pat asked my parents if they would take him. And they said yes. So Mick was reared with my family, and was always seen as a brother. Dan was still alive then, and he was pleased to take him. After Dan died, Mum carried on herself, caring for Michael.

*

When I was about eight or nine years old, I went to live in the city, in the West End of Adelaide. I think it could have been when my parents were having problems, and maybe Mum didn't want me to see what was going on. So I was taken to be with my auntie – my father's cousin. She was classed like his sister, because his mother brought them up after their mother died. They were all his first cousins, the girls, but they became like his sisters. Mum got on with them quite well, so I was left in their care.

First of all I lived with my Auntie Edith Kestel, and then with Auntie Jessie Sansbury, or Harris, in Wright Street, and I went to Sturt Street Primary School. I got to know many of the residents in the street. I used to go to the West Care family church – it was the Baptist church. Today when I see that old church, it brings back a flood of memories of when I was attending there as a child. I'd go to the Sunday school services, and sometimes the big service. Down the street a bit, a little street called Selby Street, there lived an Aboriginal woman, Ivy Mitchell, and she used to take the services in the Salvation Army church in that street.

It was good to be going to Sturt Street Primary School. I went there with the Newchurches, the Wilsons and the Agiuses. I got to know a lot of kids in the street and played with them. Maybe eighteen or twenty years ago I ran into some of the same kids that I used to play with then, and we talked about the fun times we had playing together and our fighting and squabbling down in Wright Street in the city. A lady there by the name of Betty Waller used to take some other girls and me to the West End playground. It consisted of a swing and a slippery dip, and we used to play on the equipment for about an hour, or if we were in a hurry we'd make it a half-hour. But it was fun going there because so many of us went.

Quite a lot of Aboriginal people lived in Adelaide in those days. Usually they were the Aboriginal people who had gained citizenship rights – either through marriage or because they had applied for it. They were classed as white people by the government, but really it didn't make much difference to us, because we still visited them. I didn't know much of the Protection Board in those days either – I was just a kid growing up – so a lot of that was hidden from us.

But then, as I got older, I started to realise why these people weren't living on the mission, and I started to learn about the Protection Board. You see, their mothers had married white men, so they were classed as white people. Some of them were living in Waymouth Street and Logan Street, and Trenerry Court and some in Wright Street – all in the city. They were called the West End group, and they all met there in Light Square. That square used to be like Victoria Square is today – everybody used to meet there.

When I was staying in the West End, I can remember going with my mother to the government ration depot when she came into Adelaide. It was down in Light Square, around where the new TAFE college is now. The Protection Board would give you ration tickets, and you would go down there and get the food. You couldn't go to the Community Welfare and get food orders or anything like that, because you were Aboriginal.

I liked it in the city. It was something new, and I got to see a lot more things, like going to the pictures and walking around and looking at the shops. You couldn't do that on Raukkan, because there was nothing there to see.

Everything was different in those days, even the ice-cream. I can remember my aunt sending me across to the deli – I'd go running across with the billycan to get so many scoops of ice-cream, and I'd run back, all anxious to eat it. I also remember the old ice-man coming with the big blocks of ice for the ice chests, and the coal man coming around delivering coal for the fires. And the bread man with his horse and cart, and the milkman and the greengrocer – we used to get nice fresh vegetables and fruit from him.

I remember the trams coming down the street and going up West Terrace and then out to Goodwood. A lot of people used to go out to the trots at Wayville. You'd see them all dressed up in their beads and bonnets and looking all flash, going off to the trots. They'd be racing down to get to the tram.

Once when I was only small, probably about nine, while I was staying with Auntie Edie, I lost my shoes – they were little red shoes. Cousin Josie and her boyfriend Bevan had taken me down to the playground on West Terrace this night, and when it was time to go home they bundled me back into the car and off we went back home. Then the next morning I woke up crying – I'd lost my red shoes. I couldn't find them anywhere, so Josie had to go back to the playground and dig around in the sand looking for them. And she found them all right. They were the best pair of red shoes I ever had.

While I was there in the city, I was a flower girl for one of my cousins. That was exciting, because I never knew what a flower girl had to do. It was a nice wedding, and I enjoyed it, and was very glad to be a part of it. I used to see that woman who I was flower girl for, and she often talked about her wedding. Her name was Shirley Woods – Shirley Ashton, she became. The wedding was at Norwood somewhere, if I remember correctly, but in those days I didn't know whether I was going north, south, east or west. Shirley has since passed on.

But I was only in the city for the minimum time. No questions were asked. Just every so often I was left with my auntie. I'd be there for a couple of months, then they'd come and pick me up and take me home to Raukkan. When I went back home, I was always glad to see the rest of the family, but it was always good to know that you were off to the big smoke again some day for another trip. And these trips came at a minute's notice, so I didn't know when I'd be heading back again.

*

I didn't know a lot of what was happening on the mission then. I was just a young kid growing up, and certain things your parents tried to hide from you – things that were actually going on. I didn't know a lot about the Aborigines Protection Board and the hold that it had on the mission. Being so young at the time, I guess there wasn't any need for me to know anything. But a number of different officers and overseers that came brought different rules for the mission. They were supported by the Protection Board too, because they were hired by the Protection Board. So I guess the Protection Board would have had a certain amount to do with them before they even came to the mission.

I used to see men tied up to the fence of the boundaries of Point McLeay mission – chained there. My brothers used to be among them. But I didn't know why. I found out later it was because those men had been drinking alcohol, so they were chained to the fence.

I can remember some of the mission officers. There was the one in charge when I was born and grew up – he was Mr Bartlett, old Cliff Bartlett and his wife. He was the overseer. Then you had Mr Goodhand, who was his offsider – he was a lovely person. And then you had old Sister McKenzie. She was the nurse, and she delivered me in the hospital. She left Raukkan and moved into the Aborigines Protection Board to work in Adelaide. And so did old Bartlett. After that you had Mr Haywood and his wife. Bartlett and Haywood were the two who I had most to do with. They were the ones who carried out the management of the mission. They were employed by the Protection Board as managers. They were the ones who laid down the rules, like 'no alcohol' and 'no white people to enter the mission'.

There were four teachers at the school on Raukkan. Old W.T. Lawrie was the headmaster, and Mrs Lawrie, his wife, used to do the domestics – cooking and cleaning. They lived in a little stone house opposite the store. He always took the grade seven class, even though he was the headmaster.

He taught us well, but he was very strict. He used to get your fingers and bend them right back. Oh, it hurt! He used to come along and collect your hand if you weren't writing properly, then he would hit your hand. You sure developed good handwriting, you know.

Outside of school, W.T. Lawrie went along with the old people and their discipline. We even had a curfew put on us, and if you were outside at seven o'clock at night, you got winged under the ears by him – W.T. Lawrie – and taken home and given another hiding by your parents. And next day he'd get us again in school. So we were brought up with a lot of discipline – lots and lots of discipline. But I feel it was good. Maybe we didn't appreciate it then, but I think that the discipline was given all because they cared, and that's the point I think we miss today with our young ones.

In the school classroom on Raukkan the language was all English. No Ngarrindjeri was ever talked in school. Why, I don't know. I never asked. Whether they thought we had enough Ngarrindjeri at home and around the mission, I don't know. Maybe they thought that we didn't need to have our own Ngarrindjeri language taught there. But we didn't get told off if we spoke Ngarrindjeri. No, old W.T. respected the Ngarrindjeri culture and language.

Really he was a lovely old headmaster – very strict, but very well loved by the people on Raukkan. They looked up to him, because for some of them he was their teacher too. He was there on Raukkan for thirty-seven years, I think. For all those years he reigned as headmaster, and his love for the place showed. He named his son McLeay after Point McLeay.

His son and daughter went to Narrung for schooling. They were white, and weren't allowed to go to school on the mission, because it was under the Aborigines Protection Board. Old W.T. didn't want that; he wanted them there at the Raukkan school. But he put up with it, he let it go, and they were taken to school at Narrung. They used to have a Ngarrindjeri man take them about three kilometres to school by horse and cart every morning, and pick them up in the afternoon and take them home.

W.T. Lawrie lived for years in that little house on Raukkan.

The day he left he got in his boat with Bernice and Geraldine Rigney, two sisters from Goolwa. They were returning home, and Mr Lawrie was leaving Raukkan, so he offered them a ride in his boat. To get to Goolwa he had to cross the lake, heading towards Point Sturt, and it was just near Point Sturt that Mr Lawrie had a massive heart attack and dropped dead on the boat! The two girls had to take that boat into Goolwa themselves.

They should have left him there at Raukkan, you know. He didn't want to leave, and he didn't have that long to go. He retired about 1955 at the age of sixty-five years, and I can remember we all waved him goodbye down at the jetty when he left. All the kids had to stand in two lines and wave him off. When he walked between us he was crying, poor old fella.

The school at Raukkan only went to grade seven in those days, and from there on there was no going anywhere for school – it just wasn't allowed. But once other schools became more open for Aboriginal kids, the government decided that they would allow us to go on to further education. The year we reached grade seven we were told that students who'd acquired their Progress Certificate would be coming into the city to do schooling.

I remember hearing the older ones talking about it, and they were saying that the opportunities were now there for getting a high school education, but never would they talk to us in in their language or tell us anything any more. Because they knew that the whiteman was coming.

When we all went to school on Raukkan, it meant the language and culture was safe. But the old people always knew that whiteman would come in one day and take the language, and learn more about the ways, and so nothing would be safe any more. They thought that the whiteman would take from us what we knew, and use it to benefit themselves, and we wouldn't have much left. There wouldn't be a secret – it wouldn't be just for our own use. What they were frightened of was that whiteman would take it for his own personal use. Make money out of it. I guess they saw the whitemen that were in this system only doing things to benefit themselves – not for the benefit of Aboriginal people.

The little bit that we knew, they let us keep that. But the rest of it was cut off and we had to try and learn what we could on our own. When we would ask anyone, particularly when we were in grade seven and going on to high school, we'd get told 'Shoosh! Get out! You're not allowed to hear this. We're not going to tell you anything.'

'But why?' I'd ask.

'You're not allowed to hear. Go on. Get out and play!'

That was more or less telling you, 'You're not going to learn any more, because what we teach you, you're gonna give to the whiteman.' They knew that it was coming – they foresaw that, and so they clamped up on the language. Not so much on the culture, because the culture, well, you could look at it and you could see it. But the language is very important, and that language they just would not let us learn.

Even when I grew up and got married, I went home to Raukkan and I asked some of the older ones about the language.

'No, no. We can't tell you nothing. We can't teach you anything.'

And I thought to myself, even in this day and age, when I'm an adult, they still won't tell anybody anything. It was sad to hear them say that. I did not realise then how much the people had lost. It wasn't until I went through that system myself in later years that I too learnt what we had lost.

Chapter 5

Schooling in Adelaide

It wasn't until I left Raukkan that I truly understood what it was like to live under the Protection Board. I was among the very first from Raukkan who was offered education at the age of fourteen, because I got my Progress Certificate, which was the highest that you could get at grade seven. The kids in my age group were the kids who started off getting a secondary education in Adelaide. Our older brothers and sisters didn't have that opportunity – it was never there for them, but for us it was, and the Aborigines Protection Board said it was up to us to make the best of it, which we did. Well, we tried to make the best of it.

So I came into Adelaide to live for three years. I had second thoughts about going. I didn't want to leave my family, and I wasn't allowed to live with any relatives in the city, because I was under the Protection Board system. I had to live in the girls' home. I wasn't asked, 'Would you like to come down to the city for education?' It was just 'You're going, and that's it. And we'll find a home for you to live in.'

So the next thing I knew was the officer going up to see my mother and father, and not really saying anything to me. It was said to my parents that there were no education opportunities on Raukkan, and if they would let me go, I could go to Adelaide. Mum and Dad didn't ask me nothing; they just made the decision themselves. And I bawled my eyes out. I didn't want to go to Adelaide, because I thought I was leaving my parents – that they were taking me away. But Mum said she would come to visit me whenever she could. So, feeling a little bit easy with that, I accepted the trip to Adelaide. But it was only then that I started to become aware of the powers of the Aborigines Protection Board.

So I came like a good little girl to Adelaide, and went into the United Aborigines Mission home in Parkside, at Number 4 Stamford Street. It was called Tanderra, and it was run by the two matrons, Sister Hyde and Sister Rutter. They had started Colebrook Home earlier in Quorn, which later moved to Eden Hills, south of Adelaide.

The Aborigines Protection Board paid for all our schooling, all our uniforms, and all the other clothing we required while living at Tanderra. The only great loss I felt was leaving home, because I guess I'd grown up in a protected area. And here I was, what seemed like hundreds of miles away from home – I wasn't, but it felt like it. There was no one who was really close to me if I needed somebody at any time. My aunties with whom I stayed in my younger years had died or moved to the suburbs, and they had been exempted, which meant I couldn't see them because I would have been consorting with white people. So I felt quite helpless. I bawled my eyes out, and I got terribly homesick. So did the other two girls – Pam Dodd and Elaine Karpany.

There were two of us girls taken away from Raukkan and one from near Tailem Bend for an education – there was Pam and Elaine, who were both the same age, and myself – I was just a bit older than them. We were the girls chosen out of the school, and there were three boys as well. I suppose it was a test, and we were the guinea pigs. If we became educated, then it'd be OK for the rest.

The old matron seemed pleased to have us, but getting used to our new life was a horrible experience at first. We had to learn to get on with the girls who were already living there, because they'd been there many, many years before us.

My great-grandmother
Lartelare Rebecca Spender

Grandmother Laura Glanville Harris
(nee Spender)

The Glanville site where my grandmother was born

Wurlies made from sticks and hessian bags sewn together, just as we made them for our holidays down the Coorong

Captain John Hart's Glanville Hall, Glanville

Point McLeay Mission, now known as Raukkan

Left to right: Bessie Rigney, Essie Rigney, Tokie Butcher, my grandmother
Laura Harris, Cissie Gollan, Sally Kartinyeri, Clark Kartinyeri, George and
Henry Rankine, Frank Lovegrove (senior) and David Unaipon

The dear little Raukkan Church

My two grannies Bonny and JJ with myself at Raukkan, on the site of our family home on Top Row

Di Bell and myself at the Needles

Grandfather Dan Wilson
and his brother Mark Wilson

Auntie Cherie Watkins, myself, my
daughter Leona aged 4½ and my
mother Rebecca Kumi Wilson
(nee Harris)

Jim and I

My brother Doug Wilson (left)

My brother Bert Wilson

My only son Michael Brodie

My brother Michael (Mickolo) and his grandson Isaac

A rally on the steps of parliament house

When you first arrived, you sat around the table, and these other girls would look at you as much as to say, 'You've got no right being here! You know this is our territory.' And you felt like you were really invading their territory! It was an awful feeling.

Fortunately those girls changed after a while. They got to know us, and we got to know them, and let them know where we stood with one another. Because no way were we going to let them push us around, and they certainly weren't going to let us push them around. So we came to a square deal with each other, and we got on OK. It was just a matter of getting down to brass tacks and making ourselves at home in this new place. Once we got used to it we were right. We eventually got over our homesickness.

Some of the other girls in the home were Grace Hampton, who's now deceased, and Wendy Way, Coral James and Margaret Apma. And there were other girls there like Elsa Cooper and Louise Lindsay and Janet Domasche. Janet and Louise came from the Riverland, while Wendy, Margaret, Elsa and Grace all came with the matrons from Colebrook Home when it was at Eden Hills.

Then there were big girls who stayed there like Dora Hunter. And Lois, or Lowitja, O'Donoghue, Muriel Brumby (now Olsen), and Faith Coulthard, who were older girls from Colebrook, often came home to see us on their days off. Many of the big girls came in to visit, like Amy O'Donoghue, Lois's sister. Nanna – or Nan as we called Matron Hyde after we left her care – always had a room there for the big girls. Amy and Dora were kindergarten teachers and the other girls were nursing.

The girls in the home were a lot different to me – I guess because they were brought up by the two missionaries. See, we had parents and we knew what it was like to have a family. Maybe that was something that we had to try to share with these girls, which we did, I guess, in a way.

My brothers were working, and they knew that I was in the home and going to school, and that there were things that I needed, so they offered to give me pocket money.

But Matron said, 'No. The pocket money comes to us, so we can share it around.'

But I thought: No. You're not going to get my money!

And so I used to tell my brothers to post my letters to the Parkside Post Office. I'd go there and pick the letters up, and I'd ride down to Unley Road on the bike and happily do some shopping. I'd often get underclothes for myself, because all the Protection Board ever got us was those big ugly old bloomers through government orders. But I wanted something nice, like what every other nice young girl was wearing. So I'd go out and buy nice bras and slim panties. But I'd get home and the matrons would search my school case and take 'em away from me.

One day I came back to Tanderra after school and Mum was there. I was glad to see her, but I didn't know that she'd been called down by the Protection Board. She'd come down to discuss me. They'd made a big issue out of it, and old Sister McKenzie from the Protection Board came out. She knew what time we got out of school, and she came over to the home – to Tanderra.

She talked to Mum and me, and she said, 'What do you want to do, Veronica?'

I said, 'What do you mean?'

And she replied, 'I heard you got some pocket money.'

Oh, this blooming old woman, I thought to myself. So I had to go into my room and tell them what I'd bought.

And she said, 'You're not to get the pocket money, because that's the rules of the home.'

But I remember arguing and saying, 'You know, you can't do that to me. My brother gave me that money and that's for me to spend as I want to, living in the city here.'

And I can remember her conceding, 'Oh, well, if you want to get underclothes, well that's all right – or shoes. But then you have to let us know, so we don't get them for you too.'

And I thought, fair enough. If I want to buy my own, I've got to learn to use my own money to buy things and not ask for theirs. But later I said to my mother, 'Why did I have to ask the Protection Board about everything?'

I guess I can see now why they did that to me. They wanted all the girls to have the same. And what I had, I suppose, these other girls at Tanderra thought they'd like to have too. But we couldn't have the same, because some girls did get more than others. I thought, they can't make the judgement that I have no right to have certain things because I come from a family. I guess it was just luck that I had a family and my mother and father were still alive. But, as I said to the sisters, we weren't a rich family. We weren't ever brought up to think we could have this, that and the other. I mean, we had just the basics and that was it. We were living on the borderline as it was, and we didn't have a flash house or anything like that. To us a bed was a bed, you know, and a table was a table that you sat at. My mother was a hard worker and very clean and tidy – she made it home, and so it was nice and comfortable, but we were never rich.

In that girls' home you weren't allowed to go to the pictures. That was against the rules; that was evil! So when my dear brother, who loved me so much, said he wanted to take me to the pictures to see *Rock Around The Clock*, the old matron nearly had a fit! She said, 'Oh no, you can't. It's too evil. Veronica cannot go!'

He said, 'What?' in utter disbelief.

But Matron won, and *Rock Around The Clock* was kept for another day, until I could talk my mother into taking me out. Mum let me go to the pictures, so I eventually went to see *Rock Around The Clock* without the matrons knowing.

But then slowly I started to realise that while I was there I was part of that family, which included the other girls and those old ladies. It was when I got into my second year of high school that I realised that. That second year, we had to come back early to get another lot of uniforms and blouses and undies and all that sort of stuff – socks, shoes, the whole lot – plus clothes for general wear. So, coming back, we were just like the girls the year before, looking at the new girls that had come in and thinking, well, where did you come from? What are you doin' here? They were all from elsewhere; we were still the only ones from Raukkan. They didn't get any more from Raukkan until they moved that home to another place.

You know, in the end I didn't mind living in that girls' home. Over the three years, I began to build up a respect for those two matrons. I guess it was because they respected my outwardness and the way I stood up for myself – especially with the money business. And I didn't tell tales on other girls either. I sort of just lived my life there and that was it.

But I realised that all the training that we had – working in the home, learning about the city, cooking and everything – was preparing us for our lives ahead. The matrons knew what we would be going out to when we finished our education. We had to learn what kind of jobs we were looking at, and how to look after ourselves. They knew what the city had to offer Aboriginal girls, and believe you me, it wasn't a lot!

So I was growing up in a time when I not only had to learn about living in the city, but I had to learn about living as an Aboriginal person in a white world. The matrons told us a little bit about the system, but we said, 'No, the system is not like that. We don't believe it.' But we soon learnt what the Protection Board system was really like.

We had no rights. We weren't even citizens and we couldn't vote. There were no legal services around for us to go to if we needed them. There were certain rules made by the

Aborigines Protection Board, and we had to abide by them if we wanted to go home or see our parents. And if we didn't, we knew they'd soon do something about it quick smart.

It was many years later that I realised why the old matrons in the girls' home looked after us the way they did. They showed us how to fight back without anger, because they knew what the Protection Board was like, and they wanted to prepare us for the battles we would be faced with when we got out.

*

I was at school in the city for three years. I went home on holidays, but I'd always come back. The school I attended was the Unley Girls' Technical High School, which is where the Unley Primary School is today, on Wattle Street, just off Unley Road. It was administered by Miss Maschmett, the headmistress; she was a lovely person. She must have had a lot to do with the old matrons, because she knew them quite well. She also knew the other girls who used to go there as well – the big girls. They all went there from the Colebrook home, so they must have travelled on the train from Eden Hills to Unley.

We had teachers who were very, very good and who were very understanding in the way they listened to us. If there was a problem in our work, they sat and helped us – not like some of the students today, who aren't getting that kind of outreach in education or help from their teachers. They seemed to care a lot more in those days, but I guess it was from the training that Miss Maschmett put through her school, or because of the number of Aboriginal girls who had previously gone through that school. But I give Miss Maschmett full credit. She ran an excellent school, and by the time you were ready to leave it, you didn't want to leave.

She was very happy with the Aboriginal students who had come through her school. It wasn't just the Tanderra girls – there were other Aboriginal girls who were at the Fullarton

61

Girls Home. There were those like us who stayed at Tanderra until our three years were finished and then went out to work, but after us there were little kids who came in for care because their mums were sick or had passed away. They came until other family members could take them, so they had short stays.

Miss Maschmett would never allow any racism towards the Aboriginal students, name-calling of any description, or any sort of upset. It was nipped in the bud if it ever happened, and that was it – nobody said any more or talked any more of it. It was the days of the bodgies and the widgies. The bodgies were the boys, and the widgies were the girls. We used to have a couple of widgies in our school. They were real tough characters. They had strange haircuts and styles of dress. They looked like they had just plucked their hair out of their head or their eyebrows – they were an earlier version of today's punk hairstyles. They wore skirts that came up a little shorter than average, and they really stood out in a crowd. And they'd all be down Hindley Street too on the motorbikes. These girls used to get real cocky, and a few times I saw them getting hit because of their mouths. We'd often see them in the street and they'd sing out 'hello'. They had this big image to maintain and they'd try to say something smart to you – but they were good.

It was the beginning of the rock-and-roll era – this was about 1956. The bodgies and widgies sort of led up to it. But in no part did you want to be a bodgie or a widgie – not the way they dressed and carried on! And then you had the bikies, who rode their Harley Davidson motorbikes. They were in Hindley Street and down Rundle Street – Rundle Mall was never thought of then.

That's what amazed me too over the years – how everything just changed – the progress. It left you feeling not the same about things, you know, and sometimes you wished it could stay like it was. That feeling came to me when I was looking at Unley Road the other day. Back in those days it was busy, but it wasn't as busy as it is now. You've got new shopping centres built, and there's faster cars. And to think how we used to walk down Cambridge Terrace every year on Armistice Day, and march like young ladies down the street that led to that big church, St Andrew's, opposite the memorial gardens on Unley Road. We'd wait there in line and cross Unley Road into the memorial gardens. Then we'd stand there for the Armistice Day service and sing 'O Valiant Hearts'. Whiteman has never stopped glorifying war, has he?

*

For my first two years in the city we did all the general studies like most white schools did. It wasn't any different, as far as I could see, to what Narrung or Meningie School would have had, or Murray Bridge. We did all the same exams. Towards my third year, things became more serious, because we had to start thinking of where we were going from there – what we were really going to do with our lives.

Because we didn't know much about the options in the high-school curriculum in those days, Miss Maschmett allowed the Aboriginal students a special breakdown of general and commercial studies. I did the general course, which included history, social studies, maths and dressmaking. That allowed you to go into nursing, whereas the commercial course led into office work. My friend Elaine and I stuck to the general, and my friend Pam did the commercial.

But you couldn't go on, because that was all you could do in that school – the Intermediate Certificate was the finish. The thing that Miss Maschmett was thrilled about was that all her Aboriginal students completed their course. Unley High School might have offered a higher education level then – I don't know, because we didn't have the opportunity to go on further. The Board didn't want you too educated, because if you got too educated you might cotton on to what they were up to.

We did ask why we couldn't attend Unley High School, but they just said 'No'. I guess the school fees had to be paid through the Protection Board, and Miss Maschmett may have had a lower school fee too. So it suited the Protection Board, and I guess it suited us as well. Miss Maschmett certainly had the right curriculum for us.

We walked to school every morning, and we knew the short cuts and the long cuts. Often at lunchtime we'd borrow a pushbike and ride across to Parkside Primary to see some of the younger girls that were there from the Fullarton Girls Home at the other end of Wattle Street. Fullarton was a very big home that was run by the Salvation Army, and the children there came from all over the State – Raukkan, Riverland, Point Pearce, you name it. We'd sit and have a yarn with them, or have our lunch with them. And then we'd ride back to school and return the bike to the girl we'd borrowed it from. We'd often visit those Fullarton girls, but Matron never knew that we were out of school.

I never liked the school lunches in our home, Tanderra – they were terrible. The matron made them for us. We always used to have jam and honey sandwiches, so we used to chuck 'em in the bin. Some of the other girls used to see us chuck 'em in the bin when we got to school, and they'd look at those sandwiches and say, 'Oh, we wouldn't eat that either!' So they'd share their lunches with us. I don't think I looked at honey or jam for three years after that; I stayed right away from them.

But, because we shared, we had some nice lunches some-times; or I'd save my money and buy my lunch over at the shop, or get some chips or something. The old lady that lived next door to Tanderra was called Miss Coudray, and we often used to drop our sandwiches in her bin on the way out, because we knew what was in them. She was the organist from the church we went to. She used to have a big pipe organ in her lounge, and it would sound beautiful. She was a nice old neighbour, and she never noticed our sandwiches in her bin – or if she did she never said anything.

*

One day while I was down in the home, Mum and Dad came to see me.

Dad said, 'We're taking you out on the Saturday.'

I said, 'Oh, where we goin'?'

'You're coming out to Norwood,' he said. 'We want you to meet somebody.'

I said, 'Why, who's out there? We don't know anybody living at Norwood.'

He said, 'Yes, you do.'

I said, 'Who is it?'

And my father replied, 'My sister.'

I said, 'What sister?' You see, I didn't know that he had a sister living out there.

'Yes,' he said. 'She wrote us a letter.' He said she didn't want to be known before, but she'd suddenly come to light. And that was Olga Fudge. You might have heard of Olga Fudge. She's deceased now, but they've got a hostel named after her at Brighton.

So we went out to Norwood, and my father knocked on the door. And she come down the corridor. 'Oh, my brother,' she said. 'I love you, my brother Danny. I miss you.' Then hugs and kisses, and she took us in and introduced us to Natasha, her daughter. Then we sat down and had a cup of tea. She yarned – talked and talked and talked. She said to her brother – to my father – 'Many times I've seen you on the racecourse.' But you know, she never made a move to say who she was, 'cause she was white, very fair. And she didn't want to go up and say hello. And she said she had regretted not doing that.

During the course of that conversation, there was a knock on the door – on the back door, which was locked. So my aunt opened it, and her husband, Leo, came in. And he looked at her, and he looked at us, and he said, 'Hello.'

'Ah, Leo,' she said, 'Here, this is your brother-in-law. It's my brother Dan.'

And he looked, and then he hit the roof. He said, 'Why the bloody hell didn't you tell us you were Aboriginal?' And my father just looked at her, and she was crying and carrying on.

Olga had left the mission at the age of thirteen. She worked for a white farmer at Narrung, and never ever went back to Raukkan. She lived in the broader community as a white person because of her fair skin, and she denied her Aboriginality. Leo was upset because she hadn't told him she was Aboriginal, but he quite accepted it when he knew.

Anyhow, after all that, Uncle Leo turned out beautiful. Dear little fella he was; he was absolutely lovely. How he put up with her, I don't know. It's had me beat, all these years – she was a very domineering person, you know. And from that day on, she never disowned us again, us being relatives.

So I went back to the home, really excited, telling all these girls about Auntie Olga and Natasha. When we came back from going out, the girls used to be waiting for anything we had to tell them, because they only ever went to places like church, or maybe a convention that was on. That was the only thing that the old matron would take them to. So I thought: Oh, well, I can tell you girls something that's exciting. I'll give you all a bit of news.

*

Religion was pumped into us at the home. Those sisters fed us religion for breakfast, religion for dinner and religion for tea. Then on Sundays we had it four times in one day, and that soon started to get a bit much. First I had religion on the mission, and then here I came down to this lovely home – with those two old matrons and all these girls – and there was more religion. On Sundays we went to church at the Parkside

66

Baptist Church on Young Street in the morning at ten o'clock to Christian Endeavour, then at eleven o'clock we went into the big church service. Then we came home and had lunch, and by two o'clock we were back at church again for Sunday School in the afternoon. Then sometimes we had a church tea that we stayed for, and then we'd go off again into church for the evening service. So that was church on Sundays!

It was all right for the first year, but by the second year I got tired of it. Eventually I made myself a promise that when I got out of that home, I wouldn't go to church for a good while – at least a couple of years. I was going to give myself a break.

Everyone at the church thought that we were just wonderful girls. They thought that Sister Hyde and Sister Rutter did a wonderful job with us. Little did they know what we got up to!

By the third year I was plotting to find ways of spending my Sunday-school money instead of putting it in the collection plate. We'd nick off from church and go down to the local shop. And we'd spend our collection money on lollies, then we'd take off and eat 'em. We'd buy our lollies at the deli that's still there on the corner of Young and George Street in Parkside. When we got home, we'd act as though we'd been in church – one of the girls always had a watch – and Sister Hyde would ask us how church was, and we'd say, 'Oh lovely, we had a good time.'

And she'd say 'Oh, that's good.' She didn't say any more, and we never wondered why she asked about church.

So a few more Sundays went by. You see, the matron was a patient person and if anything was wrong, I guess she had to prove her point. Then one day, it all just came down on us like a hammer! Sister McKenzie came out from the Protection Board once again, and she chatted to us and told us that skipping church and doing these kind of things just wasn't on. She said it would only cause us trouble if we didn't listen, and we could be sent to another home, and not go back to Raukkan for holidays. So there again we got that threat of not going home to our parents.

They had full control, you know. That's when I truly realised what this Protection Board was all about. I started to wake up, I suppose, and tried to find out for myself – from different ones, and older ones I spoke to – about the Protection Board.

Now, my mother and my father hadn't had a lot to do with the Protection Board, but there were people on Raukkan who had, and later, when I came home on holidays, I found it really interesting getting some answers on why the Protection Board did this and did that. And I found out that they were able to say to you, 'Hey, listen, if you don't do this you'll end up in a home.' So I decided that my last year, the third year at Tanderra, would be my last year in their control, and that was it – I was getting out of that home, right or wrong!

*

When I got to the end of my third year in Adelaide, Matron said, 'You're leaving here now. You're going home.' Then she asked me, 'What are you going to do?'

I answered, 'I've made up my mind what I'm going to do. I'm going to come back to the city and do nursing.' I said, 'In fact, I've already enrolled. They did that for me at the school, you see.'

'Good,' Matron replied. Then she said to me, 'Always feel welcome to come back and see us.'

I felt it was really good of her to make that offer to me. You see, I was starting to feel that third year of church, church, and more church was a bit much. Being young, I was getting really tired of it. It's all right for you older fellas, I thought, but we were never put up to all this church business. All I thought was, I'll be glad when I get out of here, and I'm not coming back. No more church for me. I've had enough!

But then I realised, no, Veronica, you can't say that. These two old girls have put a lot of work into you, and you have to show respect to them for it. Because they would never, ever let me down. If I asked them for something, or to do or get anything for me, Sister Hyde either got it, or she'd explain she wasn't able to get hold of it. So I thought I'd better start showing respect for them – which I did. And you know, it did get me somewhere. It got me a room there any time I wanted it, because they didn't want me to leave when I was ready to leave.

I always thought of them, Sister Hyde and Sister Rutter, when I left there. They were a real caring sort of couple. On my last day there I was crying my eyes out because I was leaving that home and leaving them. Old Matron waved me goodbye, and they were singing out, 'Come back! We'd love to see you again. Come back!' And I went away feeling real good.

Chapter 6

Fighting the
Protection Board

I was already registered to start nursing before I left Tanderra Girls' Home, so I took the Christmas break off and went home to Raukkan. While I was waiting for the Board to provide me with a uniform and other things I needed to start nursing, I decided to go to Millicent, down the South East. I had a cousin living there, and I thought maybe I could find a bit of work and live with her. I got a job in a hotel as a cleaner, but then I broke my arm in a car accident, and I went back to Raukkan to recuperate.

I'd already made enquiries about nursing in the city. At about that time the Queen Elizabeth Hospital was just opening down at Woodville, so I rang them up. But then I thought, no, I didn't want to go to the Queen Liz. I thought I'd prefer to go to a smaller hospital. The Mareeba Babies' Hospital, also in Woodville, was operating at the time, so I made enquiries there, and they asked me to go and see them. They gave me an interview, and said, 'Yes, come in. We'll take you on. You can start your nursing here.'

So I began my training as a nurse at the Mareeba Babies' Hospital, where I stayed for a year and ten months. I was there when the Queen Mother came to open the Queen Elizabeth Hospital, and was greeted by her and shook her hand.

This hospital catered for the needs of babies who suffered from congenital heart conditions, cleft palates, spina bifida and so on. But after a while I decided to try another position, so I moved on to the Royal Adelaide Hospital on North Terrace. A couple of months later I decided to leave there also and look for another job. I rang the Aborigines Protection Board to ask them – or tell them – that I was leaving my nursing job and that I needed somewhere to stay for a few nights. I was ordered to stay at the Aboriginal Women's Home in Sussex Street, North Adelaide. They were quite angry that I had left my job, and boy, did I have a battle with them over that!

That was when I really became aware of what the Protection Board was all about. While I was at Tanderra, and while nursing, I was still fairly naive about the powers of the Protection Board. I thought to myself, well, I got this job, didn't I? I was doing all right, wasn't I? But I didn't take a look around me to see how this Protection Board and its policies had affected other Aboriginal people out there. I thought I had done all right for myself. I had got a job. I didn't have to worry about the Protection Board.

But when I decided to leave my nursing job the Protection Board sure gave me something to think about! Being Aboriginal, I had to tell them everything I did, and I wasn't allowed to leave one job for another without their permission. And because I did, I was enemy number one!

Where we worked was determined by those in the Protection Board office – they'd just write you out a train ticket to your next job. They'd say, 'Here! Here's your ticket.'

'Why? Where am I going?' we'd say.

But they just replied, 'You're going where this ticket tells you!' It could be to Kingoonya way up north, or wherever they'd found you a job.

The Protection Board had heard that I was going to leave my job before I rang, because I'd spoken to others about it. I had told them that I wanted a change of jobs; that I'd like something that would allow me to travel. I'd looked at the PMG and I was interested in working on the switchboard. I thought if I could go and train for that I'd be OK. It's a government job, so I could travel wherever I wanted.

Before long I got a phone call telling me that I had to report at the Protection Board office* in Kintore Avenue the next morning. But indignantly I said, 'No, I don't.'

They just responded, 'Yes, you do. You're Aboriginal.'

I said, 'No; I'm me. You're not telling me what to do. And furthermore, what work I choose is my decision!'

But right or wrong, I had to obey them. I had to listen. They said, 'If you don't get here, we'll have the police bring you in.'

I insisted, 'Who are you to tell me what to do? I'm a human being; you can't push me around like this!'

Well, that started the first fight I ever had with them – we came to grips out at Sussex Street. You see, this was an Aboriginal women's home and the Protection Board insisted, 'You're going to stay there tonight.' So they rang the home and made arrangements for me to stay there the night. I dutifully packed my bags, and off I went in a taxi. There were two of us going to stay there – my old mate Gwen Kite and myself.

Before long I arrived, bag in hand, and met the matron there. The matron said, 'Come with me.' She had a big bunch of keys hanging on her, and she unlocked this door and that door, then another door, and through I went. Finally we met the people on the other side, who were more Aboriginal women. There was Valerie, and an elderly lady cousin, Joyce Rigney, now deceased, and another girl who has now passed on, Della Gray.

Just to look at the home it reminded me of a prison. It was awful. There was barbed wire all around the top. I said to them, 'What's all this? This is like a concentration camp.'

And they responded, 'Well, this is where they send us when we come down for medical visits or whatever.'

* The Protection Board Office was down near where the Migration Museum is now.

72

I must say that I have some very unkind memories of Sussex Street. I felt like I was a criminal when I was in that place, having to be locked in. And the old matron who managed the place – Mrs Young I think it was – had an eye on us every minute. She must have sat, so I used to think, just across in her house spying on us. You could imagine her having a spy-glass and watching you as you walked around. Once you got in, you couldn't get out, unless you went through the windows – and the matron had told us that no way was she going to allow us out. We had to stay there until next morning, when the Protection Board wanted to see us.

So after tea we were all miserable, and thought we'd have a cigarette, even though they had NO SMOKING signs all over the place. And sure enough, the matron came over, and we quickly put our cigarettes behind our backs. She started talking to us, but fortunately the window was open and the wind was blowing so she couldn't see the smoke; it was going straight out the window. But next thing, one girl's skirt was on fire. The old lady got real mad, but we did manage to put the fire and our cigarettes out!

When the matron had finally left us and closed the door behind her, I said 'I'm not going to put up with this. They're not keeping me in here.' So Gwen Kite and I climbed out through the window. Three of the other girls had already got out, so we thought we might as well join them. But the old matron saw us, and she called the police. We just got out the window and around the corner by the shops, only to find a police car waiting for us. They soon hauled us into the police car and took us back to the women's home. Then the old matron locked us in the cold old laundry, where we had to sleep on the cold floor all night without any blankets or coverings.

Next morning Mrs Angas from the Protection Board office came, and she soon laid down all the rules and regulations.

The next thing we knew, they marched us into the Protection Board office and told us we had to join the armed forces. I put up a good argument, because I didn't want to join the armed forces. That just wasn't my scene. But there were quite a few of us, and they sent us all off to the army office to sit for the army entrance test. So we all went up there, about eight of us, but on the way we decided not to pass the test, even though we were good students and had got good marks in school. So we deliberately failed our entrance test.

Word soon got back to the Protection Board office about us failing our tests, and they weren't too pleased. They had already threatened us with exemption. And that would mean that I would be excluded from my home for the rest of my life – or for as long as the Protection Board reigned. I would never be able to speak to any other Aboriginal person again, and if I got caught I would be sent to jail for six months, no questions asked.

So they ordered us back to their office, and when we got back there we found they had tickets, a bit of money and clothing all ready for us. I said, 'Hello. Where do we go from here?' And I soon found out I'd been given a new job. I was being sent north to work as a domestic. Furthermore, I wasn't allowed to go back to Raukkan, because I had failed to join the armed forces. And because we didn't want to join, we had to go wherever we were sent. Gwen got a ticket to work somewhere south, and I got a train ticket to work somewhere north.

So on the train I went. I had no say. I couldn't say, 'No; take the ticket back. I'm going home to my mother on the mission.' I just had to go on that train. It might sound like something out of a fairytale, but it wasn't. It was reality then. That's what happened to Aborigines – and that was only in the late 1950s.

I ended up on a stud farm north of Adelaide, just this side of Port Pirie, in a little town called Mundoora. They sent me there. Pat Loveridge, whose husband, George, owned the place, was nice to me. I was glad I went up there. I worked with very interesting people – lovely people, they were. They kept one pound of my wages, and the Protection Board kept my other pound. And I've never seen that money from the Protection Board from that day to this. A lot of Aboriginal people went through that same system in their employment.

I stuck it out at Mundoora until Pat went down to Adelaide one day and left me there with that blasted old husband of hers. Horrible old thing, he was. He used to become quite abusive when he was on alcohol. That day I took the horse out, you see; I often went horse-riding on the farm, but this day I rode down to see another Aboriginal girl, Liz Rigney, who was working down on Arbon's farm. So I spent the day with her.

That night it came up real stormy and windy, with rain, lightning and thunder, so I had to lead the old horse home. I led it home all right, but when I got home the farmer was waiting for me, and he abused me something terrible. He said, 'You can't take that old horse out!'

'Look,' I said, 'I brought her back safe. She's all right; she's not moaning.' But he just abused me more, so I said, 'Right. I don't have to take this from you or anyone any more. So I'm leaving.'

'You can't leave here! You're under the Protection Board!' he yelled.

'We'll see if I can't leave,' I said. So I packed my bag and called out, 'Good-bye!'

He came down the passage as I walked off. 'Where you goin'?' he said. 'I'll get the police!'

I said, 'You do what you like, but I'm off.'

I walked down to Arbon's to see Liz, and Liz said, 'Where you goin'?'

And I said, 'I'm hookin' it. I'm going home.'

She said, 'You wait. I'm comin' too.'

I said to her, 'You can't leave your job!'

And she said, 'I am!'

So she packed her bag and off we went, the two of us.

We hitch-hiked into Port Broughton to where another girl, Gwen Rigney, was working for a Dr Kelly. He was a wonderful doctor, and when we got there he said, 'You come in here and stay with us. You come and sleep here the night.'

I said, 'Well, in the morning we'll go to the policeman and he'll give us a pass down to the city.' So we went into Dr Kelly's place, and Mrs Kelly gave us a feed and made beds up for us. They really looked after us.

The next morning, Liz and I went down to the old policeman in the town there and asked him for a pass through to Adelaide on the train. Well, as luck happens, the old policeman didn't know that we'd walked out of our jobs, because if he did, we wouldn't have got anything. But we told him we had no money, so he gave us a pass each.

Then we hitch-hiked all the way to the Mundoora railway station and hopped on the train down to Adelaide. And that's where the police got us for the second time, because they'd soon found out that we'd left our jobs. When we got into Adelaide, the women's police arrested us and took us down to the Protection Board office.

Fortunately, when I walked into the office, my mother was sitting there. She didn't know what was going on, but had been in the city at the hospital with my father, who had had a heart attack – or a couple of heart attacks. She soon got the police off my back. She told them to take their hands off me, and said they had no right to treat me that way. Mrs Angas backed her up, and said that I could be released into my mother's care until she had a chance to speak to me.

Then Liz and I were told, 'You're exempt from your reserve. You're never to go back there.'

But I said, 'You can't do this to us. We've done nothing

wrong. Would you stay in a job and get a mouthful of abuse? Because I'm not going to.'

My mother and father went back to Raukkan, but I had to stay in the city because the Protection Board would not give me a pass. I don't think they wanted to let me go home because I was defiant.

'You can't stop me' I said. 'I'm goin' anyway!'

But they said, 'You go and we'll have you brought off there by the police.'

'I believe I have a right to go home, though,' I protested.

Three times they refused me a pass to Raukkan. So I went to Parliament House and I spoke to Mr Bywaters, a Member of Parliament. He rang and told Mrs Angas that they had no right to treat me like this. He put me in a government car and came with me down to the Protection Board office. He told Mrs Angas on the phone before we left that she had better have the pass ready when we got there! And when we did get there, my pass was ready all right, and my money to spend on the train – which was a five-pound note.

So that was another fight with the Protection Board. I had to battle to get home; I fought the system, and I stuck to my guns. I fought them all the way through, for policies that I thought weren't fair to Aboriginal people. It was mainly because they wouldn't do the right thing by you. But once you start fighting the Protection Board you're doing something you're not meant to do – standing up for your rights.

But the policies of the Aborigines Protection Board made some of us stronger. We fought against them and came out on top. And we went to Parliament House many times over, or to the ombudsman. We told them of the treatment that Aboriginal people were receiving under the Protection Board system, and we forced them to listen to us.

We were always looking for ways to get back at the Board. There were many Aboriginal people who hung around along the River Torrens in those days. We used to get together and we'd talk about home, and about what we were doing in the city – the jobs we'd had, where we'd been and different ones we'd met. The Protection Board used to give us a food order when we needed a feed – for an order they would put '1 pie, 1 pastie, 1 bottle of drink, and 1 packet of cigarettes'. You could fill this order in the cafeteria at the Adelaide railway station. We'd get a biro and we'd put a 2 next to the 1, so that we'd get 21 packs of cigarettes, 21 pies, 21 pasties and 21 bottles of drink, and we'd take them down and share them with all our mates on the Torrens!

That only lasted for a couple of weeks before they put a stop to it, and after that we never ever got any more for the rest of our days. But at least we thought that we got back at them in one small way.

There is a story I often tell, because it's a sad one in a sense, about three Aboriginal lads. We called them Neville, PJ and Thooky Boy and they were living in Adelaide at the time. They had been sent off the reserve as a punishment because they had been caught with alcohol there. These three fellows were given a job at the old koala farm that was just down from where the Adelaide Zoo is today. And one day the keeper said to them, 'Look, boys, you've got to look after the koala farm today because I'm going out. I expect to see everything the way it is when I come back.'

'Yes, sir,' they said.

Now, further down the Torrens there were a whole lot of us sitting by the banks of the river. All of a sudden, we saw all these animals coming along, but we weren't quite sure what we were looking at. We could see elephants – you name it – every animal in that koala farm was on the loose. There were police cars going everywhere, and people singing out. Those three boys had let the animals go.

They'd said to them, 'Go, go! You're more free than we are.

We're the ones that are locked in a cage, not you. You go!' And that was how they felt. They felt as if they were locked in cages. And that was exactly how Aboriginal people were treated then. We were counted as less than human in that system. Dogs had a better life than us.

Those boys lived with that feeling for the rest of their lives. One of those men is still living, and still he can't get that out of his mind. He still lives with that part of himself being locked inside that system.

So they are just some of the tough times that we had. I call these times today the good times – when I compare them to the days under the Protection Board.

During all that time, many Aboriginal people became conditioned. When we went to the theatres we had to go to the back. We were never allowed to sit in the nice seats at the theatre in Rundle Street and other theatres in the country. It was the same on the buses and trains – you always went straight to the back, and many Aboriginal people still do that today. A while ago I took a group of students on a bus tour of the land at Glanville, and I think that was the first time I sat on the front seat of a bus. That's how conditioned we are. When I get on a bus I go straight to the back. We were put to the back years ago by the Protection Board.

And most of us weren't allowed to vote. A few Aboriginal people were on the electoral roll in South Australia. One of them was my grandmother, Laura Glanville Spender. She was a suffragette. She believed, as a woman, that she had a right to vote, and the suffragette movement was very quick to pick up her cause.

South Australia was the first State to recognise the right for women to vote – Aboriginal women as well as whites. Grandmother made her vote stick. Even when she wasn't allowed to vote for the federal parliament, she kept voting in State elections. But younger people were stopped from voting.

No way could you put your name down on the electoral roll and line up to vote. They'd soon tell you to get out of it. If you did put your name down, it wasn't counted.

So we weren't here – we didn't exist in Australia for the whiteman, nor for the government. We weren't citizens and we weren't counted in the census. Yet during that same time it suited them to push our men out and send them off to war, even though they weren't allowed to vote. Which meant that if you went to war, but you didn't exist, then they didn't have to pay you afterwards. They fought for a country they weren't recognised in.

Much of the history of that system has never been put into the education curriculum or into the history books, because they don't want people to know what actually happened to Aboriginal people. And many Aboriginal people who are around today are products of that system, or products of the Aboriginal people who went through that system. For many years yet, I guess, we'll still continue to tell our children what happened to us during that time.

Chapter 7

How I Became a White Woman

So finally I went home to Raukkan again. I had to see my family, because my dad Dan was sick. He'd had a massive heart attack, and my mother was in Adelaide having her leg treated. My brother-in-law, Leila's husband, had had a stroke as well. He was out near Tailem Bend, and Leila was going up to be with him, so she needed me to look after her older children, and also to care for Dan. So my first priority was to head for Raukkan.

It was while I was home that Dan died, and we had the funeral service in the little Raukkan church. I guess I was happy that I had been home with him for those few days at Raukkan before he passed on.

After that I knocked around on the mission for a while, and then I decided to do something with myself. I thought, well, what will I do? I was at Narrung one day visiting the girl that worked in the Post Office there, Pam Sanders. I was good friends with her, and I decided to ask about the switchboard. I said, 'That's an interesting-looking piece of equipment. I'd like to try that.'

She saw the owner of the store and asked him if there was some work for me there. 'By all means,' he said. 'Do you want to learn? Are you willing to come down every day?'

I said, 'Yes.'

'Well,' he said, 'if you come in every day you can work the switchboard.'

Working on the switchboard was a lot of fun for me. In those days you had to put the plug in the board, and you would ring and get the person you wanted. Then they'd want someone else and you'd have to connect the two parties. It was really fun, and I got to like it. This was another job that would allow me to travel, because it was a Commonwealth job. And I did that. I made an application to move from the post office there in Narrung to the post office in Adelaide, working for the PMG, the Post-Master General's Department.

I wanted to become a telephonist. And they willingly took me in, so I was very pleased. They took me in and trained me for eight weeks in their school. At the end of that eight weeks, out of all the people in that class, I came second. So I passed the telephonist's exams with flying colours, and I thought that was a good achievement for me.

But still the Protection Board wouldn't acknowledge me or my achievement, because I'd had a fight with them earlier. If you defied them once, you lost all rights to get better help for yourself come another day. But I didn't mind. And I had passed my exams without any help from them.

So I went to Raukkan to give them the good news about my exams and tell them of my plans to work with the PMG in Adelaide. I also started thinking about the exchange down at Narrung. I thought eventually I'd like to work there again, and live at Raukkan, which is very close to Narrung. My mother was very happy, and so were my three brothers, who were home at the time, and my other brother Michael. He was only just a little fella then, and he was staying with Mum.

After I'd told my mother and everyone, I had to get back to Adelaide and find somewhere to stay if I was to start my new job at the Franklin Street exchange on time. Mum said, 'I've got a good friend, Judy Ingles, in Adelaide. She'd like you to stay with her for a while, until you find your own accommodation.' So I got Judy's number, and when I got into Adelaide she came and met me off the train. She was a very lovely lady. She took me down to the house where they were living.

I stayed with Judy for about a week, but I knew I had to have proper accommodation by Saturday night. I went three times to the Protection Board asking for somewhere to stay. Even Judy took me into the Protection Board, but they didn't want to help me. Then I remembered that a lot of the girls I knew were staying at the old migrant hostel at Woodville. So I rang up the migrant hostel and they said, 'Come down and have a chat.' Which I did. And they said I could have a room. I had to pay two weeks rent straight away, and then I was right.

I was sharing a room with another Aboriginal girl, Shirley Peasley. There was a whole lot of Nunga girls there or Ngarrindjeri girls, and that was fun. We all shared rooms.

I was glad in a way that I did my own thing and found my own accommodation – it made me stronger. Because I knew that the kind of system I was fighting wouldn't have helped me had I gone down the tube. I felt that as long as I fought for the right thing – which was for my freedom, or for whatever I felt was right – these people couldn't rule me all of my life.

And so the old migrants' shelter there at Woodville put me up, and it was great. I went to work every day to the PMG in Franklin Street, where all the switchboards were. It was fun going to work and learning this switchboard thing. One day I'd be on overseas, next day I'd be on interstate calls, next day I'd be on local calls. It was a very interesting job and I loved it – every minute of it.

One of the things I can remember most clearly was one night when a lady rang from Rome. She wanted to speak to someone in Adelaide, but it was reverse charges. So I waited for the other phone to ring, and I eventually got the fellow on the line and he said, 'All right, I will accept it.' While I was on the line, I thought I could hear rain in the background, and I said to the lady, 'Is it raining?'

She said, 'It's pouring here. It's pouring cats and dogs, to use an old saying.'

And it was. You could actually hear it teeming down in Rome. And then she says 'goodbye' after I'd connected her up to the number she wanted in Adelaide.

As I said, the jobs were very interesting – you'd get on pricings for overseas, interstate, or local. Then there was general enquiries or directory assistance to find a number. It was the kind of job that could never lose your interest. What you didn't know was that sometimes the supervisor would be listening in. You might say something silly, then all of a sudden there would be a deep, gruff voice over the line saying, 'Please don't speak like that! You are an employee and you do not speak to our customers in that manner.'

I was put into a big line of operators. The supervisor was watching us at all times, and if anything went wrong or if we said anything bad, they'd soon let us know. They never bawled you out in front of your work-mates, though. They either called you in through your line or called you into another office. It was done with a lot of tact, and they didn't embarrass you.

But outside work it was a different matter. In those days the police were shocking to us. If they saw an Aboriginal woman on the street, you were a sitting duck. One time we were standing talking to a white boy who was going back to Mount Gambier on the train. Next thing a police car pulled up and a sergeant got out, flashing his three stripes before us, and he said to us, 'Get in the police car!'

But we said, 'No!' Because I knew what the police were up to. They used to take a lot of Aboriginal women down to No. 1 Angas Street and rape them. That happened to a lot of Aboriginal women, and there are many who could tell you that story today. So I wouldn't go with them.

The sergeant said, 'Get in or you'll be arrested!'

'Arrest us if you want,' we said.

So he asked us our names, and we told him. Then he said to us, 'Right. You'll be dealt with in due course.'

The next day at work I had a visitor. An officer from the Protection Board walked through to my employer, and was asking questions about me – how much I got paid and what my shift hours were. Then I got a call through to me on my line, and the supervisor said, 'Would you please come out? There's someone here to see you.'

So then I walked out and I said, 'Yes?'

The officer said, 'We're here to inquire about you. You refused to go with the police.'

'Yes,' I said, 'Why should I go with the police?'

But they responded, 'You're just eighteen years old.'

To which I replied, 'Yes. But there was no reason for me to go with the police.'

But in those days you weren't your own boss, and what they said went!

So they kept at me, and they said, 'Well, you can't do that to the police.'

But I just said, 'Yes I can.'

I received a reprimand from the Protection Board, and was told that such an incident was not to happen again. Furthermore, I was told I would be sacked from my job quick smart!

But I was a fighter. I went back and spoke to my supervisor, and I said, 'If you sack me it should be because you don't believe I'm a good worker. So why would you sack me?'

He had to admit, 'You're a good worker. We've had no problems with you.' So I still had my job.

But it was an uphill battle after that. Once you've fought the Board, they keep coming back at you.

*

It was during this time that I started going out with Jim Brodie. I'd met Jim before with a mob of boys in Hindley Street, just as a friend you said 'hello' to. He knocked around with the boys a bit, and I used to see him every now and then. This was when I was fighting the Protection Board to get back onto the mission. I remember seeing him at the railway station with a couple of lads from home. Then we didn't see each other for about twelve months when I went home to Raukkan, but then, while I was working with the PMG, I met Jim again, and we developed a different sort of relationship. We began seeing each other fairly often.

We used to go to the Roboteria, a jukebox place in Hindley Street, with pinball machines and all that. Sitting there, joining all the rest of the gang – it was our gathering place. The young people there would be mostly Aboriginal – this was when we weren't allowed into the hotels or anywhere like that. Or we'd go to the pictures at the Majestic and the old Rex and the West and the Metro.

You weren't allowed to drink, so you had to sneak it. The Baltic people in Adelaide were very compassionate towards Aboriginal people, and they couldn't understand why we weren't allowed to have alcohol, so they'd offer to go in and buy it for us. People used to drink at home, because if the police caught you, you'd be in trouble – they'd try and find out where you got it, call you a liar, beat you up.

Then there were the sly groggers, who sold it in back lanes, back yards ... You could only go at night, when the cops weren't looking, and they used to charge us a lot of money for it. But whenever we heard of any sly groggers getting jumped on we'd be disappointed, because there your supply would have gone.

There was one flagon of stuff I remember – they called it wine, but I don't know what was really in it, because the people who drank it had bubbles coming out of their mouths – they started frothing, and the next thing you knew the room was full of bubbles! Later the police picked up some of the ones who'd been drinking it, and they said, 'What have *you* been on?'

One old policeman used to roam the Torrens River, and we

got to know him so well that when he saw us with the flagons he'd just wave his hand and on he'd go. There were some good cops in those days, and they didn't want to treat Aboriginal people badly, but that was what the law said.

Around this time Uncle Proctor – who I believe was my father, but we called him Uncle Proctor – was in Glenside mental hospital. He'd gotten ill at Raukkan from these flash-backs of the war that he was having, so they took him from Daws Road Military Hospital to Glenside Hospital on Fullarton Road. I often went out to visit him with my brother Graham. But I didn't know then that he was my father. I didn't know that for years to come.

Jim was always there when I'd come back from visiting, and he'd ask how Uncle Proctor was. Then one day Jim popped the big question and asked me to be his steady girl-friend. So I said, 'Yes.' I mean, what else could I do?

Jim had a white father, which meant that the system clas-sified him as being white, even though he had an Aboriginal mother. On his mother's side, his grandfather was a whitefella who married a full-blood, and all her children were exempt. That meant that his mother wasn't allowed to live with the Aboriginal community.

If you were exempted and you became a white person, you used to have to wear a little tag on your chest, which we called the dog-tag. When you went to a hotel or to a restaurant anywhere, you showed them your dog-tag, which told them: 'I'm not an Aborigine any more. I'm one of you, I'm white. You gotta serve me.' On it was your name and your photo – it was a little ID card, but it stated on the bottom 'this woman is not an Aborigine'. I don't know what the man behind the bar thought when he looked at me and looked at my ticket once I was exempted. He must've thought I was crazy.

It was humiliating to have to wear those tags, but that's exactly what the government did to us. They wanted Aborigines to be recognised, not for what they could do, but for how they were classed. I've often thought to myself – I wonder what went through these people's heads when they sat down to make these policies?

But Jim himself always thought he was Aboriginal, and I just thought he was an ordinary blackfella like all the other boys that we hung around with. It was only a few years before that Jim found out that he'd been given a limited exemption when he was one year old and an unconditional exemption at the age of four. But the police knew. When Jim was knocking around in Hindley Street, they'd say to the people he was with, 'You can't get around with him – he's white!'

Jim had also been in jail at Yatala for petty theft, so when we were getting around together I could have been arrested for consorting. They could have sent me to jail. The police were bastards. They hung on to the authority that the Protection Board had given them.

Jim never spoke much about his family. They were funny. They knew they were Aboriginals, but to admit it was another thing. A lot of our people who had very fair skin lived out in the white community. They didn't own up to being Aboriginal, because they found that it was easier to be white – especially when they were given a white name. It was easier to live in those days if you weren't under the system, because the Protection Board system was a terrible thing. It was a cruel system, very cruel. It did nothing for us. And you can understand why older people who could pass off as white did take the opportunity.

*

After ten months with the Post Office I discovered that I was pregnant. Oh my gosh, I thought, what am I going to do? Being single and pregnant in those days wasn't a very good position to be in. And I really didn't know Jim all that well. We had only been together for a couple of months.

I didn't tell Jim for about three months. In the meantime, I had finished up at my job with the Post Office.

When I told Jim I was pregnant, he asked me to marry him. I thought to myself, will I or won't I?

The rules of the Protection Board were that you had to go and tell them when you were getting married or engaged or whatever. And from there they always made it into a problem. But they never ever made it look as if it was their problem; it was always you, you, you and your problem.

So I went in and told Mrs Angas that I was getting married. She nearly jumped out of her chair; she nearly fell over. Then she asked who I was marrying. I told her it was Jim Brodie and gave her all the relevant information. So she said, 'Well, come back this afternoon at two o'clock and we'll tell you who you are really marrying. We'll give you an answer then.'

And I thought, gee, this must be the CIA or FBI or something. So I went back at two o'clock and I got an answer all right. They *did* tell me who I was marrying. I was marrying a white man. And the next news I got was, 'If you get married to this man you'll be white too. You'll have to give up your Aboriginality and you will be exempted for life; and you will never be an Aboriginal again!'

I looked at my dark skin, and I thought to myself, who are these people? How could they tell me that I'd become white if I married this man? But silently in my mind I thought: Good. I'd do anything to get out of the clutches of the Aborigines Protection Board. Getting exempted was a big risk to take, though. Once I married Jim I'd automatically become white. What a wonderful revelation of the Board – with the mere stroke of a pen I'd become white!

When we left the Protection Board office I said to Jim, 'What do you think? Do you think it will make much difference being exempted?' I said to him, 'You know, I just realised that when I marry you I'm going to sign my life away.'

So he said, 'Well, you've got twenty-four hours to make your decision.'

I said, 'Jim, do we have to make a decision? Do we really have any other choice? We know what the system is like. We're only young, but we've seen it all.'

Then Jim asked again, 'Do you want to get married?'

I replied, 'OK.'

And then he said, 'Yes.'

So we just walked back into the office and said, 'OK, exempt us!' and we walked out. Then we went and made our marriage arrangements at Births, Deaths and Marriages at Flinders Street in Adelaide. And that's how I became white!

*

Jim and I got married in the Registry Office on 6 October 1961. My brother Graham came along, as well as my mum and my brother-in-law, Jim. My sister Leila was sick at home. After the ceremony my Auntie Edie Kestel put on a big spread for us in her house at Woodlands Park. Her husband, Uncle George Kestel, gave me away. Bethel Wilson (now deceased) was my bridesmaid. At 2 p.m. I walked into the Registry Office Aboriginal. At 4 p.m. I walked out white. I call that a classic!

So for four years I was a white woman. I had many white friends in those days, and I'd ask these girls, 'If you married an Aboriginal man, what would you become? Would you become Aboriginal?' And they'd just look at me and laugh.

And I'd say, 'Well, it's not as funny as you may think. In fact, it's quite serious!'

Many Aboriginal women went through that, but it leaves scars on you for sure. It leaves you angry, and it makes you racist. And believe you me, we had plenty to say about the Protection Board and white people in those days, because they segregated us from the rest of our family – they split us up.

But being made white didn't make much difference to the way I felt. I said to the Board, 'What are you making me white for? The colour don't rub off.' I still felt Aboriginal, and I still mixed with my own people in the city. But the system did make life very difficult for my family to visit. You see, there were consorting laws that said a white person (like the new me) could not consort with Aboriginal people. So that meant I could no longer speak to my mother or brothers or my sister – because they were Aboriginal and I was white! And that was very cruel. In fact, legally I could not speak to any Aboriginal people.

The permit system still existed in those days too, which meant I had to get special permission to visit my own family at Raukkan. That was one of the worst aspects of the system. If you were exempt, you had to have a good reason to visit the mission or reserve, and even then permission was often refused. So, when I married this so-called white man, I had to get a permit to visit the mission.

But at about that time, Grandmother Glanville fell very ill. She was sick home on Raukkan. Then one day Mum came up and said that Grandma had been brought into Northfield Hospital because she'd had a stroke. Grandma was in her eighties then – she would have been about eighty-six years old. Mum often came up to the city to visit her in the hospital, so we would quite often visit grandmother in hospital too. My sister would also come up from Raukkan and visit, as well my brothers, who worked on the railways, so that was good.

Grandmother was in the old Northfield Hospital, where there were a lot of Aboriginal girls working at the time. There was some employment scheme between the matron there and the Protection Board. They employed so many Aboriginal girls there that grandmother and another old fella, Uncle Rowley (Uncle Henry Rankine senior), thought they were just outside of Raukkan. It was sad really, because they didn't realise just how far away they were from home. But while they thought Raukkan was just around the corner, it kept them alive. Then they realised that Raukkan wasn't so close, and they began to fret.

It was a great loss when we got the phone call saying that Grandma had passed away. But I think Mum was relieved in a sense, because she wouldn't have wished Grandma to live on with a stroke, being the big woman that she was. She was in pain most of the time, so it was best for her that she did go when she did, much as we loved her.

When they held Grandmother's funeral down at Raukkan, it was very hard for me, being white, to attend. I had to go and get a permit for myself, a permit for my husband and a special permit for my new baby – my eldest daughter, Margaret. Once we arrived at the mission, the officer in charge made it his business to come up to Jim and me to tell us that if we weren't off the mission immediately the funeral was finished, they would take our baby daughter away and we would be sent to jail for six months. So we had to move off the moment the funeral had finished. We didn't even have time to say, 'See you, Mum!' nor time to say goodbye to my brothers and sister. That's how they got at Aboriginal people – they threatened to take away our children. A lot of children were taken away in that system.

It was those sorts of things that caused me to develop a hatred for that department. Not for all white people, but for those white welfare officers in that department that carried out those policies.

I've seen them take children away. There's a man living in Adelaide today who still remembers seeing his mother kneeling on the road at Raukkan screaming as she watched him being driven away. He was standing up on the back seat, looking through the back window of the car, as he and his brothers and sisters were being taken away. And he said to me once, 'I can still see my mother.' She's dead now, but he can still see her on that road. So a man nearly in his fifties has had to live with those memories all these years. Those are the sorts of memories a lot of those Nungas who sit in Victoria Square today have.

The way Mrs Angas treated us was a classic example of the type of authority that the Aborigines Protection Board had over Aborigines. Later, when people asked her why she did that, she would say, 'Yes, but we had a job to do!'

Many years afterwards, I'd see her around town. She'd been very ill over the years, so whenever we met I'd say 'Hello.' And she'd ask how different ones were going, and I'd tell her.

But she said to me once, 'I feel very sorry today for what I did.'

And I said to her, 'You didn't have to do it. You didn't have to stay there and issue those policies, and take away the children, and do all the things that you did! Because you made a lot of Aboriginal people hate you. Now many of them can't take that hate back. It's been too many years. Some of them feel sorry for you, but they don't want any more to do with you. You say you want to come back and be our friend. But how can you be that after all that you've done to us?'

And I could see the remorse on her face. The older ones would speak to her, but they wouldn't spend much time with her. It was just 'Hello. See you later,' and that's it. She would have loved them to stop and have a yarn, but the hurt is still there.

Chapter 8

Family Life

After Jim and I married we lived around the city for a while. Jim continued with his job in the foundry, and eventually got a position as a driver. We lived for two years at Torrensville with Nana Bugg, an old lady who had boarded Jim before we got married. It was while we were there that we had our first child, Margaret. Nana Bugg had another old lady called Alma living with her, and they were beautiful knitters. They knitted everything for Margaret – a full layette.

Margaret was born in 1962; then we had Colleen, who was born in 1963, and then Michael, who was born in 1965. Then after that we had Kathy in 1966 and finally Leona, who was born in 1968.

They graded my kids when they were born as if they were grading fowl eggs. My first two girls were graded differently – Colleen was declared one-eighth Aboriginal, while Margaret, the oldest one, was declared one-sixteenth Aboriginal. You see, Margaret was quite fair, but Colleen was a little bit darker-skinned. They both had the same parents, so it just goes to show how silly the system was. Only Margaret and Colleen went through the Protection system, not the others.

After Grandmother died, Mum no longer came back up to the city as much, so I didn't see her as often as I wanted to. Jim's mum came over once, though. That was the first time I met her since we'd been married. Jim's sisters were already here in the city – Colleen and Noreen. Colleen had worked in the hospital at Ceduna, but she liked coming into the city. So she was here with Noreen, and his mum Naomi Brodie came over to visit. She came from Port Lincoln, where she was living at the time, although she was reared up over at Penong, west of Ceduna on the Eyre highway. Jim was born in Penong, but he was more or less brought up in Streaky Bay.

Jim's mother was a frail little woman; a nice little woman. She was separated from her husband, Mick Brodie. I believe Mick was a bit of a taskmaster to get on with – very, very tough, and set in his own ways. He was Irish, but he was born in Cape Town, South Africa. Jim's mum stayed for a week in the city and then went back to Port Lincoln.

After two years at Torrensville, we moved and got a house at Thebarton, and we stayed there for a year and a half, I guess. We sort of moved around a bit in those days, but one of our moves was because of a scare we had with our first little girl, Margaret.

Margaret was not quite two years old at the time – she would have been about sixteen months. She was a pretty little girl and had this lovely curly hair. She used to wander a lot around the yard, but this particular day she got out of the front yard. There were a few visitors there – lots of relatives. When it came to my family or any Ngarrindjeri people visiting me, Jim and I defied all the Protection Board's consorting laws and invited them in. We were sitting down yarning and having a great old time, so we didn't notice Margaret had gone. Then all of a sudden I noticed that she wasn't there. My sister went one way and Jim went another, and I went another way and my cousin went another way. But nowhere could we find her, so soon we started to panic.

'Oh, blow this!' I said, 'We're not getting anywhere!'

And just then Jim happened to walk past these Italian people's yard, and he could hear a little voice on the other side of their fence. So he looked over the fence, and there was Margaret, sitting on this great heap of sand and throwing it up in the air – having a wonderful time, she was! Jim picked her up and growled and smacked her all the way home. I think it was the mere fact of making us panic in our search for her that made him so angry. But he soon got her home and got over his anger.

After that we found another place up in town, in Carrington Street, but it was the worst place that we could have ever moved into. It was a haunted house! One night Colleen had woken up for her bottle, so I got out of bed to go downstairs. This image of a woman was standing there. At first I thought it was my brother's sister-in-law who was living with us, so I said to her, 'If you're going to the toilet, I'll follow you downstairs and wait for you.' So I followed her down. But when I got to the back door, I realised the woman I was following wasn't human. She was a ghost! It was like a block of ice hitting me. I had this icy-cold feeling all over me. And whoever says your hair stands on end when something like that happens, it's true! This image was so real, I still find it hard to believe it was a ghost.

I quickly went back inside, into the kitchen, and started getting Colleen's bottle. Then something made me go outside again, and I saw the woman was still there, but then she disappeared before my eyes!

A detective came around later and asked if anyone had seen a woman in the neighbourhood.

I said, 'I haven't seen a woman, only a ghost.' When I described the woman I'd seen, the detective said that a girl who looked like that had recently died next door, in the very next house! We moved out the next day.

After that we moved down to a nice little house in Brompton. We had been living in Brompton for some months when Mum came up and told us that she was also moving into a house in the city. After about 1961 the government started offering homes to Aboriginal people to come and live away from the mission, and later they offered Mum a house in Athol Park. She thought she would give Adelaide a go, because Raukkan in those days didn't hold much opportunity for people. Most people were going away to live. Employment opportunities were better elsewhere, as was education. And of course at that time Raukkan was still under the authority of the Protection Board system, so they still couldn't buy alcohol legally, and there were other restrictions.

My two brothers decided to come into Adelaide and help her with the move. Between them they had twenty-five years of employment up their sleeves with the railways, so they were due for long service leave, and were able to come and give her a hand. It was good having Mum in the city, though we still had certain restrictions on us from the Protection Board, like the consorting laws, and that made it hard for us.

Our son Mick came along while Jim was working for some construction people who put up scaffolding in the city. We were still living at Brompton then, and Michael was born at the Hindmarsh Community Hospital. I had a most surprising birth with him. I'd been in hospital because there was something wrong with my potassium levels, and I was planning on going home that morning. Then all of a sudden he just came – the doctor couldn't believe it. But he was a healthy baby and was born very naturally – no medication, no nothing. It was just a natural birth, and that was good. But he was born in the summer and it was stinking hot. In fact he was born on the 8th of January, on Elvis Presley's birthday, so his birthday was easy to remember.

Once we'd had Margaret, Colleen and Michael, Jim decided to go and work on the railways. So we headed for the South East when Michael was just a toddler. Jim went ahead and got the job, then he told us when he was ready for us to move down. We moved to a place called Frances in the South East, very close to the Victorian border, just four towns down the line from Bordertown. It was a nice little place. There were two Aboriginal families there, and the boys used to come in and visit from all around – shearers, other men working on the railways and so on. We stayed there for a while, but when I was pregnant with Kathy, I didn't have such a good time. I had pneumonia and ended up in hospital in Victoria, because you had to go over the border for medical treatment. But I still came up to Adelaide to give birth – I eventually had Kathy at the Queen Liz.

I returned to Frances for a while after Kathy was born, and then we moved to Tailem Bend, where we lived in a Railways house. I stayed home looking after the children, like most of the other women whose husbands were on the railways. We had the child endowment to help us, but it wasn't much in them days. Jim was still working for the railways, which was good while it lasted because he could at least get a fair earning. Some of the Aboriginal men working on the railways then were under the permit system, which meant that each time they left the mission they had to get a permission pass from the superintendant, the big boss, to return to the mission. This was so no one could come and go at random and break the Protection laws.

Other Aboriginal people living in Tailem Bend were exempted like us, but our own community never kept away from us – in fact, there were more people from the community coming to us than ever. Men working up and down the line would come and talk to us. The rellies were always there, coming around drinking – as I've said, we grew up acknowledging our relatives and sharing with them. The police there never bothered us – but if they'd known how many people were around, we would have been in jail! After all, the alcohol ban was still in force. Albert Namatjira bought alcohol for a relative and was jailed for it.

But I didn't think that was our life, particularly when we

got to Tailem Bend. I eventually got tired of all the drinking, and I decided to get out. Jim had had an accident at Tailem Bend and wound up in hospital there. He met with some boys one night, and thought he'd have a feed of chooks. He punched the chook house with his fist, but ended up cutting it open on the wire, and eventually got blood poisoning. I left him in Tailem Bend hospital to come to stay with Mum at her place in Adelaide. But then they had to bring him up to the Adelaide hospital to operate on him. When his hand started to heal after about fourteen days, he came home.

In the meantime, I'd decided I wasn't going to leave the city any more. Mum had settled into the city by then – she moved in 1968 – and my sister had also moved into Adelaide a couple of years later. It was lovely to have them both living there. I could pop over and see Mum whenever I felt like it. There was never any fear any more, because the referendum was held and the Protection Act was finished. Jim and I were Aboriginal again, and so were our daughters.

When Jim got out of hospital he said, 'Well, I'll get a job, and we'll get a house here.' But it never eventuated. We were always living with Mum, or with his mother, who had moved to Adelaide from the country.

Times were really tough. We didn't have any dole payments, and we couldn't go to the white community welfare to get any money or anything. There were no hand-outs. If you asked for hand-outs, they'd take away your kids. So my survival in the city in those days came, I guess, from some of the tactics I learnt from surviving during the Protection System.

You see, life to us in those days was being in a family and being close. Today I think a lot of that is gone – it seems like those who aren't doing so well are jealous of the ones who are. It's sad to see that happening. I often say to my son-in-law, 'I didn't bring my children and the grandchildren up to be jealous of one another, but to always love one another and to share with one another.' I guess that's what we would like to see happen to our children too, because we grew up like that. Myself and others in the same age group had that closeness with our families, and even when we ventured into married life, we still kept that. And today we've still got that closeness – it's a bond, and we'll always keep that bond till we're no longer on this earth.

But I don't know if we can say that for our younger kids that are living today. They do have that bond with people of their own age as they grow up – which they may keep until they've got to our age. But some of them may not even see the age of forty or fifty, with their drug abuse and alcohol.

*

After they made me white when I married Jim, it really made me stop and think. That's when my involvement began in looking at the policies that the Aborigines Protection Board had set up for Aboriginal people. Jim and I found strength in fighting that system together in those early years of our married life. It made us stronger.

But when the Protection Board wiped out my Aboriginality and declared me white, life was still much the same for me living in Adelaide. Once I was made white, I could legally vote. But I didn't. I thought, 'You're not going to get my vote.' My husband didn't vote, so I wasn't going to vote. And anyway, as far as I was concerned, I was still Aboriginal.

Yes, there were many of us who went through that experience of being exempted. Some of them it did affect, and some of us it didn't. But thank God I was only made white for a little while. I don't know what would have happened if I had been made white for twenty years. I would have been devastated. In fact, I might have got used to being white, and argued against being made Aboriginal again. Who knows?

Officially Aboriginal people weren't even here in Australia – from day one of federation in 1901 until 1967. If you were

Aboriginal you weren't counted in the national census, nor were you allowed to vote. And we couldn't consort with white people, nor drink in a hotel, and we even had to get permission to get married.

Then everything seemed to change at once – bang! The Labor government came into power in South Australia in 1965, and Don Dunstan became the Minister for Aboriginal Affairs. The Protection Board had already been abolished and replaced by an Aboriginal Affairs Advisory Board and Dunstan started a lot of other changes. He also brought in laws against racial discrimination in 1966, so that we were able to walk on the same side of the street as white people, and that we could sit anywhere we wanted in the same picture theatre as white people. And that we could go into a hotel and have a drink. He ensured that we were no longer living under a system that carried a stigma.

After segregation in the theatres ended, we went and sat right down the front, to see what everyone else had been seeing. There was this odd feeling – we had these rights now, and what were we going to do with them? I also tore up those little tickets that we had to wear on our shoulders – the dog tags that existed to say we weren't Aboriginal.

It was afterwards that I saw a lot of problems arise, because of people not being educated about alcohol. Before it was legal, there was some domestic violence associated with alcohol, but nothing like there was afterwards. Women also drank a lot less then – so how could non-indigenous people tell their adopted children they were adopted out because their mothers were drunk?

Then the 1967 referendum came round and we were finally counted as Australian citizens. Afterwards, this letter came saying, 'Dear Mr and Mrs Brodie. We are writing to you to inform you that you are once again Aborigines. You are therefore eligible for any benefits there are for Aboriginal people.

You can come into this office and make your claims for whatever is due to you and your family.' It was from the Department of Aboriginal Affairs, which had assumed the powers of the Aborigines Protection Board.

When we got that letter, we went into the office to see them. But, you know, it didn't really make much difference to our lives. It couldn't. They'd conditioned us over the years, and it wasn't easy to change our thinking about ourselves overnight. When all these electoral notices came out to us, telling us that we could now get on the electoral roll, a lot of Aborigines didn't want to vote. They said, 'Why should we? They didn't want our vote before 1967, so we're not going to vote today.' I refused to vote – a lot of us did. There was a lot of us who had gone through the same sorts of humiliating experiences.

I hated white people then, but I don't hate any more, because I realise now that the people who made that system were sick. They had to be, to expect human beings to live under a system like that. And the traditional people were often treated worse than us on the mission. At least we had a home and a roof over our heads.

I mean, we had government people in the Northern Territory who wanted full-bloods to be tattooed! Do you realise that Hitler's system of tattooing the Jews came from what they wanted to set up in the Northern Territory? If we consider the apartheid system in South Africa, where did that begin? It began in the Torres Strait Islands. It's a real eye-opener, isn't it, to think that your own country was the source of two such terrible things? So you can imagine the kind of system that the Aborigines did live under back in those days.

A lot of kids were taken away from their families in those early days too, and many of them were adopted into white homes. But a lot of those kids have come back to their Aboriginal families today. They've come back very confused and brainwashed and asking lots of questions.

One night a young Aboriginal woman sat down with me and she said, 'Those kids that have been adopted out and have skin as black as black – how can they live with white people and think they're white?'

Well, what I say is that it's not really the skin that was looked at. It was all in the mind, and many of them were brainwashed into thinking that they were white.

But, as I said, some of those kids that were taken away have come back now to their Aboriginal families. Some have got themselves into university and are doing tertiary studies, and apart from their general studies they are doing Aboriginal Studies. These are the Aboriginal kids who are trying to find their identity, and with the help of their relatives they're starting to get back on their feet. Because when they were adopted their birth certificates were changed, and the names of their mothers and fathers were changed. Their birth dates were also changed, and their real names were changed, in order that those kids could never ever find their way back to their Aboriginal parents if they were still alive. So that just goes to show what sort of a cruel system it was.

*

Shortly before my youngest child Leona was born, Jim and I parted company, because Jim went off to live with someone else. I moved a couple of times, and eventually found an Aboriginal Affairs Department house in Osborne, where there were quite a few Aboriginal families. Further down the track I found someone to live with too, but that didn't last long. I got rid of him and tried living on my own.

After Jim and I split up and went our own ways, I got involved in other things. About 1970 I became an Aboriginal Education Worker for the Taperoo Primary School.

There were quite a few Aboriginal children at the school, including my kids, and there was a lot of racism, with the white kids calling the Aboriginal kids 'black' and 'nigger' and stuff like that. I had a talk with the headmaster. I said, 'Look, maybe we can break down some of these barriers if I start Aboriginal cultural classes.' The headmaster was all for it and helped us in every way he could.

I had already been involved in Aboriginal art classes, and so I was able to ask a lot of people how we should do the Aboriginal awareness program. The job involved teaching Aboriginal culture to the white kids in the school, and our own Aboriginal kids joined in too and had a great time. The emphasis was on doing things and telling stories, and I found a lot of the kids came along. We used to paint the kids up and they'd make spears and boomerangs. We used to show them how to build wurlies, and it was like a big cubby-house to them. And I'd tell them stories, and get other Aboriginal people to come in and do things with them. They'd also tell them stories and show films, and take them out to different Aboriginal communities and other places to look around.

It was an exciting job working with the kids and doing things with the school committee and the school in general, as well as with other Aboriginal people in the community. I worked with my mother and Auntie Cherie Watkins, and we did some Kaurna cultural studies with the kids. Mum took Auntie Cherie and the kids and me down to Taperoo Beach and showed us how to cook meat in the traditional way. She remembered from when she was a child seeing how her grandmother used to cook the food in the reeds. She showed us how to pick the right reeds and make a fire, and then put the reeds on top. When they got hot she put the meat on top of that to cook it. Now, whatever was in the reeds I don't know, but she put all the meat on that and then covered them with another lot of reeds, and it turned out absolutely beautiful. She also made damper in the ashes in the lovely white sand, and that was nice too. The kids enjoyed their feed of meat with damper and butter and golden syrup. They thought it was a real treat. Even the Mayor of Port Adelaide joined in.

Doing those cultural classes helped stop the kids from calling each other names and fighting, and the white kids came to understand a bit more about Aboriginal people. It was a very new thing for that time. When the other schools heard what was going on, they wanted to know how they could get in touch with Aboriginal speakers as well. Soon there was a regular round of speakers talking to the schoolkids, telling them how the Aboriginal people themselves were brought up. It was the only way you could get kids to feel how Aboriginal people felt and lived, being in the city.

Today's cultural awareness programs are different. They bring up so much more emotion. The time-lines are being shown, telling what actually happened to Aboriginal people years ago, so finally you can bring out all that muck that for years you couldn't speak about, because you never knew what the government would do to you if you did. With the primary-school kids, we couldn't talk about that side of things. You could bring in a little bit of it with the high-school students, but you had to do it gently.

I just got myself involved wherever I could. I was involved with setting up an Aboriginal complex to house Aboriginal projects, but unfortunately it never happened. I was also in the very first intake of students at the Aboriginal Community College, and I also joined the Friendship Club of Port Adelaide. A white chap called Peter Bicknell started up a friendship club in the Port, and all the young kids from around the district went along. Their parents also took part, as well as their grandmothers. It was fantastic to see the roll-up of kids on a Sunday. It was fun, and the parents were able to join in with whatever the kids were doing.

It was during that time, in 1973, that my mum died. Coping with her loss was very difficult because we were very close to one another – and even more so as she got towards the end of her life. Not long before she died, I was able to reunite Mum with her cousin Dolly Abrook, who had separated herself from us for many, many years. Dolly's son had died, and I went to the funeral in place of Mum, and just Auntie Dolly seeing me at her son's funeral was enough to make her realise that she badly wanted to see Mum again. So I took her to see Mum and she got a real surprise. It was wonderful to see them sit there and yarn. They had a really good time together just before Mum passed away.

The sudden loss of Mum, and studying at the same time, became a real heavy burden for me. Things started to get me down, but I kept on with the course I was doing at the Community College, seeing I only had twelve months left to do. Then from there I stayed at home, and I didn't do any work for a while. It was then that I began to drink – not real heavy, but heavy enough. I shouldn't have been drinking at all, because I had the kids, and I was living on my own.

But then I decided to get involved again with the cultural side of things. We were still working to get an Aboriginal cultural centre, and we travelled around the countryside looking at different places, seeing what others had done, and what we could do. I even went to Canberra for a week, and while I was there we worked with these high-tech blokes from some government department. We discussed with them the Aztec Indians and their homes, and the way they built them, as well as the Pueblo Indians. Some of these blokes had been over to America to look at these Indians. You see, their culture was very similar to Aboriginal culture in some ways, so it was interesting for me to be doing all that. But that only lasted for maybe three or four months.

When that was gone, it left me at a loose end, and I didn't work for a long time. I guess it was for a year or two. And then my brother Bert died. That's when I hit the drink more, and I began to go right downhill. Even though I thought to myself, 'This is not good. I better stop this', I couldn't. I tried to, but I couldn't stop. So I just went with the flow, and ended up very, very ill.

I think it was only by the grace of God that I pulled through those years. Something happened in my life – I don't know what, but after I was brought to my knees with alcohol and reached rock bottom, I started to come up again. And those who come up and stay up win through, but those who don't ever come through either die during the process, or they're a long time getting there. And then by that time a lot of brain damage may occur.

It was during my time of recovery, during those very first weeks, that I experienced a spiritual awakening. And that awakening was something that was meant for me, because since then I've never looked back.

Chapter 9

My Spiritual Awakening

There is one other very dear member of my family who I should pay tribute to, and that is my late sister Dorothy Leila Rankine. Leila became very well known in the Aboriginal community in Adelaide and was a highly respected woman in her own lifetime. She was a very wise person and a very learned person.

Leila was my only living sister. I never knew another sister, because they died before I grew up, or before I was even born. So I loved Leila dearly. Now Leila was a wise person, because she used to listen to the old people a lot. She had a very strong love for her land – the Coorong or Kurrangk – which she called 'the land of her father's people'. In fact, that is where Leila chose to have her ashes laid – at Panmurung Point, which is near Ngarlung, where we used to go as children every Christmas holiday. Leila also held strong memories for Hindmarsh Island, which is the land her father always visited when he went hunting for swan eggs.

Much of Leila's early life was spent growing up and living on Raukkan. She was much older than me, and when I came into Adelaide for further education Leila continued living back on Raukkan, because she was married by then and starting her family. So over the years she lived with her husband Jim Rankine as a family on Raukkan. But two years after Mum moved to Adelaide, Leila decided to move as well, because Jim's health was very frail at the time and she thought it would be better to be nearer to mum if she needed help.

As it turned out, moving to Adelaide did a lot for Leila. I believe it opened the way for her. She became active at CASM – the Centre for Aboriginal Studies in Music. She got to love her work there with the late Dr Catherine Ellis, and with other people from Adelaide University. She had lots of work to do there – all associated with music, whether it was taping music or whether it was getting involved with the Pitjantjatjara people who worked there. Leila saw to a lot of the needs of some of the young Aboriginal students that attended CASM. Some came from interstate, and many from here in Adelaide. She became the chairperson, the mediator, the auntie, the mother and the counsellor to all of the students there.

When I was really down after Mum and Bert had died, Leila was very good to me, and through her I got involved in CASM. So I developed an interest in music, and learnt to play the violin and cello. At this time, my alcoholism was getting worse. I finally decided, through the help of a dedicated doctor, to kick the alcohol habit.

I had six weeks at Robinson House at Hillcrest. Going there was very scary for me, as I didn't know what was happening to me. My nerves were all shot to pieces, and my body was absolutely soaked with alcohol. I will always be grateful to the friends who helped me through that time – Val Power, who virtually saved my life, and Uncle George Tongerie, and the late Neville Smith, who sat with me throughout the tortured nights of drying out before I was able to enter Robbie House for treatment. Then at Robbie House I met Dr Peter Goldsworthy. It was largely due to him and these other very special people that I stuck with my rehabilitation program. Without them, I would have surely died of alcoholism.

The road to recovery was very hard for me during those first two weeks. I just couldn't see my way clear. I always thought that God would do it all for me and I wouldn't have to do much myself. How wrong I was! Then I took a good look at myself. I realised that if I didn't do something for myself fast, I would lose my children. I didn't want that – I had done enough to them already. One night, before I went to sleep, I prayed to God to please help me and bring me out of the throes of alcoholism.

After my prayer I cried, and then I settled for sleep. The next morning I awoke with a surprise – I had slept all night and awoken to a brand new world. I felt different and I could see things differently. What had happened to me? I ran to the phone box and rang my sister and her friend, as well as my cousin Dora. I could not believe the change in me. Leila said she would come and visit me, which she did, and we cried together. The psychotherapist saw me and immediately confirmed that I had had a spiritual awakening. From that day to this, I have never looked back – nor lifted another drink to my mouth since 1979.

When I stopped drinking, I did my twelve steps with Alcoholics Anonymous. I'm never sorry that I did, because they are the ones that keep my life in order – particularly the inventory. If you can't do that inventory about yourself, then you're not a person. The inventory tells you the mistakes you've made in your living, and if you don't follow that, you'll find yourself turning back to the drink again. Over the years I've seen many do that.

The twelve steps, you know, are important to the ones with the drinking problem *and* to their families, because you can also include your family in those twelve steps. Your family can support you. That was when Leila came into it with me, you see. She came to Hillcrest to visit me, and she knew I was on the twelve steps. She made an effort to come out to a meeting on a Friday night and to listen. It made me feel good, and I'd see others there with their families who would come out and sit and enjoy the twelve steps session with the AA program. And you'd see them going away happy and smiling. The idea of the twelve steps to me is in that saying: 'God grant me the serenity to accept the things I cannot change, the courage to change the things I can, and the wisdom to know the difference.'

That's how it made me feel when my sister came out, or when one of the kids came out to see me. It gave them a chance to see what I was trying to do and what I was trying to achieve. When you've been an alcoholic, there are things in your life that you never ever want to do again. The program makes you fully aware of the things that you did do, and you feel ashamed to know that you did these things.

I think one of the most exciting and wonderful things about me sobering up was that I have still got my friends. I've always had good friends and thoughtful friends. They will never come near me if they've been drinking; but after they've sobered up they'll come and see me. And that's been for the whole time I've been off the drink – they've never deserted me. If I go to a party, they might say to me, 'Oh, look, we're gonna have a drink. Is that all right?' But I'll say, 'I don't have to answer for you fellas, like you don't have to answer for me.' And I'll also tell them, 'But you've got to answer to yourself in times to come if you are going to have a drink.'

You see, I've got a husband who drinks, and I can tolerate his drinking. But as long as I live, I will never pick up another drink – and that's the important part of the program – knowing that you will never pick up another drink. I wish I could do that with food!

But your life goes over so many rough roads when you're drinking. I often think of people in speeding cars when they are drunk. You hear the reports come on the news, and you remember, years ago, when we used to speed around in cars. That's when we were charged up, and we did it all under the influence – we didn't care. We could've been dead ten times over; yet somehow something kept us alive. And that question will always come up – why not me?

So we learn from our experiences, and we keep on learning the older we get. Our young ones today – we hear them say how hard life is for them. But I often wonder, if younger people had had our lives to live, what would they do? I could not imagine it. I could never, ever imagine them living the kind of life that we did under the Protection Board system. They'd never survive, because they wouldn't know how to. It was very difficult, you know. It's no wonder that it sent some of us to the drink!

*

Another member of my family that I must tell you more about is my dear son Michael. I didn't say much about him before because he's been gone for twenty years now. We named him Michael Daniel Brodie, but we called him Mick, and he was a lovely lad. Very tall, and a very handsome-looking boy. He was born between my four girls – he had two girls ahead of him as well as two girls behind him. And, as much as he loved his sisters, they fought like mad at times. Then one day he fended off his older sister, Margaret. She couldn't believe he had such long arms and was able to fight her back. After that she didn't hit him any more – nor did Colleen. But they shared a lot of time together with him, and they loved him as any family would love their only brother. He adored his two younger sisters, Kathy and Leona, and always cared for them.

Mick loved swimming, and he used to dive off the jetty at Brighton and swim out for what seemed like miles. He had really powerful limbs – very strong arms and long legs. He just loved the water, so he'd swim and swim and swim. Then at the tender age of sixteen he was gone, from injuries caused from a car accident. It was a very sad time for us, because we never thought we would lose anybody so young in our family.

It was during the year before we lost him, that a crew decided to make the film *Wrong Side of the Road*. We took part in a lot of talk and negotiation about the film with Graham

Isaac and Ned Lander from Sydney. Mick was around long enough to take part in this film, which was good. It was lovely to see him up front there in the film. But little did we know that Mick wouldn't be with us next year. And so that film is something we've got there now that we can always watch and look back on. In it you can hear him having his last little say there – I can still hear that old voice talking.

You see, unfortunately, Mick got tangled up with these boys who were into drugs and alcohol. The night of the accident he was at a party, or on the way to a party or whatever, and in the process a car was stolen. He was in that car, and this car hit the light pole on the corner of Tapley's Hill Road and the Old Port Road. It was a Saturday night, but it was after midnight so it would have been on a Sunday – the 10th of May, Mother's Day 1981. It was one o'clock in the morning, and the car rolled and Mick was thrown through the windscreen. The cut that he had to the back of his head severed the nerves in the base of his head. The hospital said he was brain dead. He never ever regained consciousness.

He was on a life-support machine in the hospital for a short time, but I took him off it. I didn't want him to live on to be a vegetable. At first I didn't want to take him off it because I thought he might regain consciousness. But as the day went on, things just didn't go right with his body, and so when doctors called us back in there, I had a big discussion with the neurosurgeon, and I decided to take him off.

But Mick's life was good. He lived in many different places and he had lots of mates and girlfriends; and he had his sisters and his Auntie Leila, whom he loved dearly. His lifetime had a lot of little interesting snippets – especially with his cousin Brenton, Leila's son.

I remember when Brenton thought that he was very smart because he'd grown some lovely green plants amongst his tomato plants – I don't need to tell you what they were! But he came home one day to find that Mick had pulled every one of them out. Well, Brenton started behaving like a raving lunatic, but he could never lift his hand to his cousin Michael. He and Mick had something special between them. They had a bonding as if Brenton was an older brother, because Mick didn't have a brother, you see.

And so Mick was loved very deeply by Brenton, and Brenton tried to teach him a lot. Of course Brenton wasn't on the right side of the law most of the time, so what he taught him wasn't always desirable. But whatever he taught him, Mick thought it was good. We'd just say to Brenton, 'Keep Mick on the safe side,' and we believed that he would.

Yes, Mick was loved very dearly by us all. Lots of his mates remember him, and even though it's been twenty years now, the memories haven't died down. They've just got bigger and better. So that's been really good for us because we've been able to get over his passing, but we always feel that he's still around us.

Dora Hunter, or Auntie Dora as Mick called her, loved her nephew – she always had a lot of time for him. Mick used to call her his topper-upper, because he always caught her down by the beach. He'd say, 'Auntie Dora, have you got twenty cents?' or 'Have you got forty cents, or a dollar?' And he was always running up to Auntie Maggie and kissing her on the cheek. So he had his special little ways with our older ones – he had lovable ways. The girls still hold him in the highest esteem, their brother, because he gave a lot of love to them. They're always telling his little nephew JJ what their Uncle Mick was like, and they also tell the girls, Bonnie and Tasha. And they listen.

And Colleen's boy Troy would ask a lot of questions about his Uncle Mick. When Troy was about four years old I took him up to the cemetry with me one day, and he said, 'What you doing here, Nan?'

And I said, 'See there! Your Uncle Mick's buried there.'

114

He said, 'Where?'

And I said, 'Under all that dirt there, under the ground.'

He said, 'Really? I want to come back here later on.'

I must take him back one day. We'll do a bit of cleaning around the grave and get it all set up nice.

Mick's buried in the West Terrace cemetery with his Uncle Bert. And whenever I drive past that cemetery I always call out and say, 'Hello Mick. How ya goin'?'

You know, Uncle Bert used to call him his king when he was growing up. And Kathy was Uncle Bert's princess, while Leona was his birthday girl – because she was born on his birthday. So he had his little names for those three. But 'his king and I' – I always say, 'The king and I are buried together.'

We have lots of good memories of Mick, and we don't hurt any more for his loss. But we know where he is. And you know, Mick must've been special because we often talk about the king of music – and that was Elvis Presley. And Mick was born on his birthday. He thought it was great having a birthday on the same day as a celebrity. So I guess Mick is closer to Elvis than what we are today. He must be sitting up there with Elvis, and listening to every concert put on with Elvis's music. Yes, Mick would be sitting up there watching with him. So now each day we live we think of him, and we have a good laugh about him.

*

Jim and I didn't part as bad friends, so it was easy to say 'Hello' or 'How you going' and stuff. I guess that was the result of our long partnership. When Mick died, Jim came over to see us, and we didn't chuck him out the door or anything. We let him in because we understood that he was grieving too.

So here I was, a couple of years later, coming along in leaps and bounds with my new-found independence, when all of a sudden Colleen said one day, 'Mum, can Dad come back to live with us?'

I must have turned on her, because I said, 'No, I love my independence.'

You see, I didn't want to lose that. But then I thought, well, it won't do any harm I suppose. But I decided to have him back under certain conditions. So Jim came back, and we are both happy now.

Today we still have our own beds, but we're more compatible now and more friendly. I don't think I could ever hurt anybody and be cruel and say, 'Get out!' You see, Jim had been good to us over the years and provided well for us, and looked after us. He always kept a roof over our heads. Even though we didn't have much in those early days, we survived together.

Chapter 10

The Aboriginal Sobriety Group

After I gave up drinking I continued with my music for maybe six or seven months, but then I felt that I had to take my message of recovery to others, so to speak. So I took a month's work with the drying-out clinic at Osmond Terrace. That job was very interesting, because I came across many, many sad cases and I gained a real insight into what this disease of alcoholism can do to people. A lot of Aboriginal people attended that clinic, but many times they would sign themselves out. The end result was usually more alcohol and often excessive use of alcohol, which eventually brought them back again, or they died.

What was very rewarding was to be able to get some of them to consider rehabilitation, because I knew from experience that it was not an easy thing to do. Many don't want to give up their drinking, because they believe they will lose a lot from giving it up. In actual fact you don't – you gain more – but until you experience that, you don't ever know. So during that time I saw many alcoholics that I knew come and go from the clinic.

When my month at Osmond Terrace was up I went back to CASM. But I still wasn't satisfied; I wasn't settled. I've got to be where the alcohol is, I thought. I've got to go among it and work among it, because if I lock myself up in my house away from it all, I'll never know if I'm truly cured.

Leila was wonderful. She was there for me the whole time I was rehabilitating, and it was wonderful to have her around.

She came and got me and said, 'You can't live in your house all the time. You must get out.'

So out I got, and the very first thing I had to do was to walk past the hotel. I know it really worried Leila, because she was thinking, 'What will she do?' But she didn't have to worry, because I discovered that I felt horribly sick with the smell of the hotel. I knew then that I'd never go back to it.

While I was still drinking, Basil Sumner and his brother 'Moogy' from the Aboriginal Sobriety Group had invited me to meetings and set up a support program for me. The group had been going for quite a while, but Basil, who was a reformed alcoholic himself, really got it sparking. He wrote submissions to set up soup kitchens, to fund new premises, to extend the group's programs, and to employ a female field officer. When I came out of Hillcrest, Basil and his brother inspired me to keep going. I was employed as the female field officer, and Basil offered me a job looking after the soup kitchen in Pulteney Street in the city. He was quite young – younger than me – and he was great to work for.

We used the back part of St Paul's Anglican Church there. We had many kitchen helpers cooking the big pots of soup and looking after the drunks who came in off Victoria Square. We listened to many, many stories from them. From the old ones I'd get a good laugh. The minute they walked in the door they had the utmost respect for the workers. But I'd also hear heartbreaking stories from the old alcoholics – Uncle Keith Karpany, Dicky Appleton and many others. They were lovely old people, because as they got older they mellowed, so it was easy to talk to them and listen to the stories that they had to tell. They'd tell us about their wanderings and their experiences. There was one fella, Jack Keith (Karpany) who used to do tricks with matchsticks, and with twenty-cent coins. They'd also talk about their families and how they missed them.

The Anglicans eventually did us a real disservice with the soup kitchen. First they decided to sell the stained-glass windows in the building that we used, and then they ended up selling the whole blasted place. They wanted money, and they certainly didn't want to put it back into Aboriginal people and their problems. Money meant more to them than people who needed help. They left as soon as that place was sold, and we were told we'd have to give up the soup kitchen. I thought it was pretty greedy of them, you know. It was mean to kick us out, because it was a really good program, and they left us with nothing. It dampened our spirits, and I went away from the church after that.

The Sobriety Group was left without premises to cater for the needs of the 'square people', as we called them. While those premises were there, it gave us a place not only to feed the alcoholics but also to entertain them, because we had many entertaining afternoons. But the soup kitchen finished there and then, and the Sobriety Group never carried on any-where else – at least not like the one at St Paul's Church.

I also had the opportunity to work with Father Tony Pearson, who was a Catholic priest who worked with Aboriginal people. He worked at the Other Way Centre, which was just around the corner from the soup kitchen. He was the chaplain to work with Aboriginal people and he also visited the Yatala Labour Prison. I often went with him to visit different Aboriginal men in Yatala. I would go up to A Division and chat with the boys up there. I'd see how they were going, and ask them what kinds of things they were doing, and what was happening for them with their education and training and so on.

While I was there, I met Max Stewart, an old fellow who was accused of murdering a young girl in Ceduna. It got a lot of media coverage at the time. I had many long talks with him, and he said then to me, 'I never killed that little girl.' He said, 'A whiteman done that. I'm doin' time for what somebody else did.' But he also said, 'That man'll get caught up with one day. He'll get found out.'

He was such a gentle person to speak to, and I could never imagine him killing anyone. You can always tell a person who's done something like that, by either his talk or his ways, or his eyes – something will give him away. But Max Stewart looked like someone who was straight down the line. He told me all about his mission, just east of Alice Springs, and how he was longing to go back there. And I believe he is back there today, and is a leader among his people.

After the soup kitchen closed, Basil offered me a job at the Sobriety Group hostel at Alberton. It was the first ever Aboriginal women's hostel for rehabilitation from drugs and alcohol, and I was the Sobriety Group's only female field officer. It was a very new thing and very exciting.

The women in the hostel were mainly young, some with children, some without. I still think of one girl who was there. She was a beautiful girl, very pretty. She stayed there with me for about two months, then the next thing I heard she was murdered up in Queensland. It was a terrible pity. She could have been anything she wanted to.

I looked after traditional women as well. Some of them had been stabbed, and other times I'd get calls from someone who'd had hot water thrown over them. The emphasis at the hostel was on self-help. The more serious cases – people with serious psychological problems and so on – had to be referred to detox clinics. It was a good job for me, because I was in contact with so many women, and that was a support for me. We kept in contact afterwards as well – they were all Aboriginal women, and we'd see each other around.

But at that time we were held back by other organisations, with their rules and regulations, as well as by funding problems. For instance, the Sobriety Group wanted to get lovely furniture for their hostels, because when you had women clients, you liked them to move into nice premises with nice furniture, so they could feel as if life was worth living again. We wanted to give them some meaning in life and reason to go on staying there. But we were only a third-party hostel within Aboriginal Hostels Ltd, and they really didn't take much interest in us. So we only had the bare essentials to work with, which made it very difficult.

While I was working at the hostel, Leona lived with Leila at Mitchell Park, and Kathy and Colleen were with me in a unit at St Mary's. At first I went in to work from there, then later I took up quarters in the hostel. After about five or six years of living at the Alberton hostel with the women, I was moved down to the men's hostel at Maude Street, Glandore, for a time. They didn't have anyone to manage the place, so they found a temporary replacement for me at the women's hostel, and I went down to the men's hostel.

At least at the men's hostel there was a bit more decent furniture, and I had a nice kitchen to work in. I also had a lovely open fireplace, so I didn't feel too badly off. The hostel was haunted, though. It had a little ghost living there, and sometimes you'd hear it play the guitar. It was quite scary if you didn't know it was there, so we never really told anyone that came into the hostel. We just let them come in, and before long they would hear it, whistle, and we'd just say, 'Oh, that's usual.'

The men at the hostel weren't allowed to drink on the premises. If they had a drink, they had to leave. It was amazing how many of them would say the same thing: 'If I give up drinking, I won't have any friends.' They couldn't see beyond that barrier. Each time someone died of alcohol or drugs, they'd say it was never the abuse that killed them – it was always something else. Even though they'd become very remorseful when someone died, they wouldn't admit what the problem was.

I'd been at the men's hostel just over twelve months when I became sick. I did lots of coughing and I became very weak and soon found out that my cigarette smoking wasn't helping me much. Even though I wasn't all the best, I still kept blaming myself for the way my chest was rather than blaming the cigarettes – because I still wanted to keep on smoking. So I did just that – I kept on smoking! Then one night I found myself losing my breath, which forced me to take a trip to hospital. After a long examination, they told me that I was asthmatic. And I said, 'No way. I'm not asthmatic, and I'm not giving up my cigarettes!'

The doctor said, 'You keep smoking and you'll be back in here in three weeks, and then you'll see what happens.'

But he was wrong. I wasn't back in three weeks – I was back in two weeks with a very nice relapse, and it was all through the cigarettes.

Once I heard that I was a fully fledged asthmatic, and once I heard the terms of managing my condition, I threw my packet of cigarettes in the bin. But it didn't take long for one of the boys who was living at the hostel to dive in on them!

I stayed at the men's hostel for two years, then they called me back to the women's hostel at Alberton.

Chapter 11

A Visit to India

In 1988, just out of the blue, I was asked to go to India. It was through my work with drug addicts and alcoholics that I was offered the trip. Basil Sumner came to me one day and said, 'Look, I've been offered this trip to India, but I can't go. So I would like you to go instead – I know you are the right person for such a trip.'

I said, 'To where?'

He replied, 'To India.'

I was so taken aback I said, 'What?'

So he repeated himself, 'I want you to go to India in my place.'

I couldn't believe my ears. It was like a dream come true! India was a place I'd always read about; and a place I was interested in because of Gandhi and his works. I'd read Gandhi's books and followed his journeys, and I was very interested in this little man who had done so much for his people. So when I was offered this chance of a lifetime to go to India I jumped at it, and said 'Yes' straight away. There was no way I was going to knock an offer like that back.

Community Aid Abroad had offered five of us this study tour – there were four other Aboriginal people besides myself. We were to go over to look at the poor communities in India, and see how they had developed themselves. These were people who had nothing, and they were trying to develop themselves to a point where they could get themselves and their community going again. None of the higher-caste Indians would help the lower-caste Indians – if anything, the higher castes took away from the lower castes if they thought what they had would help them.

The high-caste Indians showed their higher-up-ness in the way that they spoke and walked and the way they stared at us. And if you were seen talking to a poor person, you didn't get very nice looks from them.

The idea of the trip was that a group of us were to have a chance to see the workings of the poor Indians. There is a name for them – the Harijans – and it means children of God. That was a name that Gandhi gave them. They are very lovely people, and very humble people. They work tirelessly from morning till night every day, and what they earn in one week is less than what you and I would get paid in one day! It was a lesson for us to see people work so hard for very little.

Even the children – little ones, you know, are working in tea houses on the roadside and have to go on the big trains when they pull in to try and sell goods. You see little children crippled or maimed, crawling along the train aisles selling goods to make a few bob for themselves – just a bit of money to try and keep their parents going. And you see old women, who haven't got sons, living on the streets, and nobody cares how long they stay there. They stay there till they die – that's the way the family structure works. If you have a son, you're lucky – the son will take you into his home and look after you. If you haven't, then no one worries about you.

My visit to India was good in many ways, because it forced me to evaluate my own life and my own source of food – it made me look at my whole self. After that trip I said, 'If I don't have a loaf of bread, or if I miss a meal, I won't grizzle and I won't gripe, because those humble people in India have taught me that.' They taught me never to be selfish. Many of them didn't have much to give, but they did! The poverty that we saw there was a real blow-out to us all – we just couldn't believe it. But as we travelled from community to community, and as we met more and more of these poor people, we suddenly became a part of it. And when the time came to leave India I didn't want to go.

We travelled through many cities and smaller communities, but we started our trip in Delhi. From there, we flew to the overcrowded and dirty city of Calcutta. That city was a horrible culture shock to us when we first arrived. As we drove into Calcutta in the taxi there was this great big hill, and we thought there were birds fighting on top of the hill.

We said, 'Oh, look at the birds over there fighting one another.'

The Indian guide pulled the taxi up and he said, 'Get out, get out! Look!' Then he said, 'Do you know what they are on that hill?'

We said, 'What?'

He said, 'They're people, and they're on the rubbish dump. They're fighting the birds for the food scraps off that dump.'

We stood there and we burst into tears – we just cried. All over the dump we saw men, women and kids fighting the birds for food scraps, and the whole place stank!

And we also saw kids swimming in water that was as green as green, and the smell of the place was terrible. It was unbelievable, most unbelievable. But until you've been to these places and you see the poverty there, you would never believe what these people go through. The hygiene there is very bad, so that's why they warn you when you go to India to only drink water out of a sealed bottle – like Coca-Cola. We were that full of Coca-Cola by the end of our trip we were fed up with it!

I also visited Mother Theresa's homes for children in Calcutta, and that was a beautiful experience. She did a wonderful job in Calcutta in her children's homes and in her home for the destitute and dying. It just about broke our hearts to leave all those little kids behind, knowing that their parents didn't really want them. We were saying that if there wasn't so much red tape, we would have brought half a dozen kids each out of the country, but we sort of had to hug them and love them and then say goodbye. We came away feeling sad at heart for these children. Calcutta is a bad city – you even see very young girls on the street prostituting.

To be taken away from the horrible scenes of Calcutta was quite a relief. They flew us down to Boobanashwa, where we stayed in the most beautiful hotel for a couple of days before going further south to a seaside resort.

And there on the Bay of Bengal, in this little seaside place down south, we saw the most wonderful sight I had ever seen. It was early in the morning, and they told us to get up and to go down to the beach. So we got up and when we got down to the beach we looked out at the ocean, and we saw there were about five hundred fishing boats out there. It was unreal. The same boats came back that night, and each one was filled with fish, so they poured the fish all on to the beach. And it was an amazing sight – the whole beach was alive with fish. The women were very busy and they would run with their baskets on their heads, then pick the fish up and off they would go to sell the fish in the village. There was a whole process going on, and eventually the whole beach was cleared of fish. It was something my eyes would never behold again in a hundred years – unless of course I had the money to travel backwards and forwards to India.

We also went to see their temple, but they said to us, 'Don't go too near the temple because the keeper of the temple will come out in a minute.' So we stood and watched and when he finally came out we saw that the keeper was a huge gorilla – he looked after the temple! He is let out each day by these people, and he walks around the temple to see that everything is all right, then he goes back inside and they lock the gates. It is only then that other people are able to go inside the temple.

Then they took us up to the mountains, still in the south, where the Tibetans lived. They are such beautiful people – so humble. And their village was spotless. You could eat off their chook-house floor; that's how clean it was. When the Chinese hit Tibet, these Tibetans moved out and came to India to live, but they found the middle of India too hot to live, so they went south to the highest mountains and built themselves homes there.

We saw the weaving that the women do. They were so generous, so kind, and the foods that they cooked us were absolutely beautiful. We saw these noodles hanging on the clothesline when we arrived, and we wondered what they were. Then, come tea time, the old men who did the cooking for us came and brought the noodles in for us, and they were the most beautiful noodles I have ever tasted. It was nothing like I'd ever tasted before. I'd like to get the recipe to make that taste one day.

Everybody was so humble and so nice that you didn't feel like coming home. Sometimes I get a yearning to go back to India, but now my health has broken down a lot more than when I was there.

I've met people who have been back to India three or four times, and I've asked them, 'Have you been to this place and that place? Have you seen this or that project? Have you seen any of these people?' But they haven't. A lot of them travel over and just go to the ashrams to stay for a while. I've even thought to myself, well, one day I might get back to one of the ashrams there. Yes, it would be good just to see India again.

In that fishing village, different communities would buy the fish from the women, and the money would be put straight into a bank account, which they would build on. A committee would sit down there and discuss how one particular family didn't have a house. So they decided, 'OK, we'll build them one'. But they told them that they've got to help; they've got to be there and have a little input too. And if they get any spare rupees then they've got to contribute maybe one or two – they're happy with that. And so they'd set to work and they'd built them a house.

That's how they worked. There were no arguments – they just got on with the work. And they were happy in their projects, such as building homes, because they were doing something for others.

As we travelled throughout India, we looked at various projects that were started from next to nothing, and I said to myself, 'This is what's got to happen with Aboriginal people back in Australia. We've got to go back and give these ideas to our own people. We've got to tell them that you can start from nothing.'

Do you know what the Indians said when we told them about our situation in Australia? They said, 'Why don't you kick the English out of your country?'

I responded, 'Do you know how big Australia is? Do you know how many English there are?' I said that in Australia it would be impossible for us to do that, as we, the Aborigines, are the minority.

But I have to say that my people sometimes don't know how lucky we are. Even though we have got what we think is a rotten government from time to time, we're far luckier that those poor Indians.

Next we travelled north to Bodgaya, to the city of the temples, and that was something you'd never see anywhere else. We actually went to see the giant Buddha. There's a turn that you take to walk up to the Buddha, and when he came into sight we looked up and saw him. He was so big, I couldn't believe it. But we couldn't touch him – the guide said that we couldn't. And lined up along the walls there we saw some people with leprosy, which was really sad. They were begging and they definitely needed something, so we didn't mind giving a few rupees to them.

I think one of the things that had a big impact on us at Bodgaya was the way we were looked after there. But our train ride from Bodgaya back to Delhi turned out to be very interesting because, unbeknown to us, a lot of Sikhs had got on the train on the way through. The Sikhs had been fighting a separatist movement against the Indian government for many years – in fact, when we arrived in Delhi there was a big uprising. The Indian guide who was with us could under-stand what the Sikhs were all saying among themselves, so he sang out to us, 'You stay here. If you want to go to the toilet, you tell me first.' It was quite scary.

Then these Sikhs came down to where we were on the train and they just stood there and stared at us. We said to each other, 'Oh, help! What are they going to do with us?' But the guide told us that when they were talking, they were saying in their language that we resembled the Indians that lived in India. And we thought, well, that may keep us a bit safe for a while. And it did. They were amazed that we were from Australia, and they thought, how could they be from Australia when they look like the Indians from here?

It was lucky we only had light carry-bags, because when we got to Delhi we had to run. All our guide said to us was, 'Run! Let's get out of here!' So we ran up the steps as quick as we could to where the taxis were, and we just got to the taxi when we heard the gunfire start. The Sikhs had opened fire and killed many Indians that day in Delhi.

When we got to the YMCA where we were staying, the police immediately took our passports and locked them away, because of the uprising. They were frightened that the Sikhs would pounce on every place that had tourists staying, and that they'd come into the YMCA and take our passports. They could have climbed in high windows by using ladders, so we had to keep our windows closed. It was so hot at the time – 46 and 48 degrees Celsius – and we nearly cooked, even though we had the fan going. We just wanted to leave the windows open, but as soon as they saw us open them they said, 'Shut your windows.' So we'd try to go to sleep or lay down in the lounge with those big wind fans on.

Before we had to return to Australia, we had a whole week of touring around Delhi and nearby areas. In Delhi I went and visited Gandhi's tomb and sat in Gandhi's garden and meditated for two hours. I just sat there – it was wonderful. It was very, very spiritual and I felt at home.

We had a look at the Taj Mahal at Agra, which was the most beautiful place to behold. The prince who built it must have thought very highly of his wife to build such a mausoleum. And we saw the jewels in the wall, in the tomb, and quite a few were missing. Outside the Taj Mahal they had little monkeys doing tricks on bikes for the tourists, and they had cobras dancing up out of their baskets to this pipe music. We were lucky they had their teeth pulled out or I wouldn't have been there. No way!

They also took us to the Moghul temples to look at the holes that were left in the pillars that once held the diamonds which the British had taken. And they showed us where the Kohinoor diamond – the one that still sits in the Queen's crown – was taken from. They said, 'We still want that one back, and we'll get it back one day.'

Then from there we went back to Delhi, where a beautiful meal awaited us at the YMCA. The Indians were very good to us, but they certainly didn't like the British, not at all. They never had any time for them. They still feel the hate for what the British did to their country. When we returned from the Taj Mahal, a busload of British tourists came in to where we were staying. And do you know, the Indians totally ignored them!

These people were standing there saying, 'Look, we want some help,' and the Indians just walked straight past them as if they didn't exist. Then those same Indians turned around and said to us, 'You come with us. We don't want to help those people; not yet.'

But we told them, 'You know, you have to learn to live with all this – like we did. You can't hold hate any more.'

We visited some beautiful spots in Purri, where the British had the guns pointing out to the sea. They've now made that into a beautiful restaurant, and they were so proud of it. But as soon as we sat down they'd come and sit at our table, while we were trying to eat, and tell us the history of what the British did with this beautiful place. So we were trying to eat, but were getting fed all the hatred about the British. We just looked at one another and nodded at them saying, 'Yes, yes, yes.' But we eventually got to understand why the Indians felt the way they did. They constantly told us about the British and what they did to them. If you know what the British did to the Aborigines in Tasmania, and to the convicts, well, they were just as cruel to the Indians. And the Indians were adamant that when the British left India they'd rebuild again – that was in their minds daily – and that's what they've done at Purri.

When we were in Purri they took us to see the main temples there. I saw the big Hindu temple and I walked inside. Fortunately I did have a scarf on my head, so they must have thought I was one of the Indians going in. The temple is so beautiful. When you kneel down and look up you can see through to the sky – you can see the stars, and it's almost as if you're worshipping in an outside church. The Indians take pride in their art and the way that they have designed some of their temples and buildings.

While we were in Purri we went to the bank one Saturday morning – John, Margaret, Lucy, Panini and myself – and we were waiting to cash our traveller's cheques when some trouble started. Next thing in came the police or the military with rifles, and they started telling the people in the bank to hurry up. So I ran to the counter. The fellow there knew that we were from Australia, and he sorted out our cheques. So then we grabbed our money and took off through the door and headed for our hotel.

But I loved India when I was there. It taught me to be grateful for what I had, and not to grizzle about what I didn't have. The people there were so humble, so kind and so beautiful. The money that's needed in that country is huge, but if you're prepared to go there for a reason and learn, you'll gain a lot. The humbleness of the people above all seems to get to you – the whole way through. I was sad to leave India, and I vowed that I would go back one day.

Chapter 12

Work in the Community

After I arrived home from India, it was back to work again at the Aboriginal Sobriety Group – back to the hostel. But it was never the same. There was something that I missed. Looking back now, I think I was missing India too much. Things weren't as nice as they seemed before. For example, the food didn't taste the same, because while we were in India we had some absolutely beautiful food, and when I got back home the food that we eat here seemed so plain. In a way, I think I fretted for India.

I did go back to work with the ASG, but after another year with them I decided to stop work. So I did just that and went home and rested for a while. I felt like I needed a break. Then a year later I tried for a cooking job that was going at Kuri Yerlo, which is a community centre down at Largs Bay on the Le Fevre Peninsula, cooking for the children in the kindergarten there. So I applied for the job and I got it.

By this stage my kids were all grown up – but my kids were always made to pretty well look after themselves. I already had grandchildren, because Troy was born to Colleen – he's my oldest grandson and was born in 1981 – and then in 1984 Natasha was born to Kathy. She's the oldest granddaughter.

At Kuri Yerlo, it was fun doing something for children and working with children – looking at their likes and dislikes of certain foods. Just being there seeing the kids come into kindy each day was a real experience for me after working with adults for so long. Quite often I would have a couple of little ones sitting at my kitchen table having their breakfast, because they didn't have time to have breakfast before they left home. And they'd talk to me and tell me little stories, and I quite liked listening to these kids telling their stories. One little boy there would often hit me with a few great big long tales, and they were quite remarkable for a child – he had such a vivid imagination. He used to tell me some wonderful stories, and I used to say to him, 'One day you'll read your story in a book.' But it looks like it's me who's going to read *my* story in a book!

It was good to be there with these children, and being able to talk to the workers. I spent two and a half years with this job. I saw all sorts of problems with some of these children. I think one of the saddest things I ever saw while I was there was when some little ones lost their mum – she passed away, and she was only a young girl. Apparently she had bad kidneys but she didn't know it. She was a pretty girl, and she left behind four little children. There's a lot of kidney disease among Aboriginal people these days.

Sometimes I'd go into the kindy while the kids were having their lunch, and they'd sing out to me, 'Sit by me, Mrs Brodie. Sit by me!' Then eventually I got called Nanna, so it was, 'Nanna! Come and sit here, Nanna! Nanna, come and sit there!' So Nanna had to spread herself around in the kindy room, and the kids loved it. And I knew that they appreciated what I cooked for them, because children are great tasters and they'll tell you whether they like your food or not! They're the best judges of the lot, and yes, I passed their test.

Ah, and their drawings were wonderful – they'd do a drawing and I'd get one to put in the kitchen. So the kids thought of me in that way. And whenever they had a whole lot of stuff given to them, like biscuits or sweets, they'd often come into the kitchen and say, 'Here, Nanna. This is for you!' So they were thoughtful little children, and it was fun for me.

But then illness got me. By that time I was ready to give up work, and in a way I was glad. I had to do lighter work, because I'd been on my feet most of the day and I had developed more trouble with my rheumatoid arthritis. So my legs didn't really take to walking around and doing all the things I had to do in the kitchen – lifting things and mopping floors. You see, for six or seven months I was the cleaner of the whole place as well as doing the cooking – so two jobs in one didn't hit off too well. First I had to give away the cleaning and just stick to the cooking. Then I decided to give it all a break and have a rest.

After I resigned at Kuri Yerlo I took up more committee work, where I felt I'd be more use, especially after I'd had a break for a while. The doctor wouldn't let me work anyhow, so while I had time to get on to these committees I did. Along with other Aboriginal people, I helped set up The Parks Aboriginal Health Unit, and that was good, because we needed an Aboriginal service in that area. They have now got a diabetic clinic going there as well. It was quite a different kind of setup to the Nunka Warra Yunti centre – the new Aboriginal community centre on Wakefield Street in the city. That new centre is a bit like a showplace now, and it doesn't have the same community feeling that The Parks has, or its old building further up in Wakefield Street. It's a comfortable feeling there. You can go to The Parks and feel relaxed and enjoy a cup of tea and have a chat and see a doctor or whoever's on duty.

I'm still involved with that committee, and I'm involved with the Aboriginal Housing Board, even though that's a headache sometimes. Not a lot of people understand that you must keep that roof over people's heads. If you lose that roof over your head, then you're in deep trouble.

Originally, years ago, Aboriginal Housing was set up to accommodate Aboriginal people so they could cope with living in the city after moving in from places like Raukkan, Point Pearce and Ceduna. But now it seems it has got out of hand in some ways, because some people try to use the system. They said once too that they'd never ever evict Aboriginal people, but it's like everything else I suppose – you can make these rules and regulations, but trying to apply them is another thing. So the housing has become a blasted headache, believe you me. There are days when I dread going into those meetings, but I end up going in because I know certain Aboriginal people won't get help if I'm not there. So I'd better go – I have to voice my opinion.

I'm happy to help people, and I'm not frightened to talk to different ones if I think they need to speak about their housing situation. I guess a lot of them are glad when someone from Housing can go out and speak to them, because they don't get a lot of communication. The housing managers are there, but they cannot talk to their clients on the same level as we can, because they're not Aboriginal. And some clients believe that the housing managers have airs of superiority about them. But that's not it; the managers have their jobs to do.

So being involved with the housing, and also with the Aboriginal Sobriety Group, keeps me pretty busy. ASG is very important to me. That's my most important committee of all – I'll never ever become a defunct member of that committee – simply because of all the years that I've believed in it. And today I still believe in it. I believe that you must have total sobriety to be able to tell others not to drink or not to use drugs. Basil Sumner gave me life membership of ASG.

Leila and I were also involved with Warriappendi School, which is an alternative secondary school for kids in the city who are having trouble fitting into mainstream schools. In fact, they now have a shield called the Leila Rankine Shield, which they present to the most outstanding sportsperson at Warriappendi School each year.

While Leila was working at CASM, she developed diabetes, which was very sad because it's a dreadful disease. I'm a diabetic myself, but I'm not as bad as Leila was. It affected her eyes, and I think her heart as well. But she coped with it. Then at one stage she had an operation, which I think did more harm to her than if she'd battled through with her diabetes. Maybe she would still be alive today if she hadn't had that operation.

Four years later or maybe five, Leila came down with diabetes again. This time it came back with a vengeance, and Leila never really recovered. She became very ill with it, and it held her back from doing the things that she loved.

Leila kept working for as long as she could. Towards the end, when her kidneys gave out and the pain was too severe, she felt that life didn't hold the quality for her that she should be having. She just couldn't go on. So she begged me to let her go, and I said, 'Well, if that's your wish I'll let you go. But I'll be here if you need me.' So between her daughters, Auntie Maggie, and a dear friend Gloria Sparrow and myself, we made Leila's wish possible.

And one other person I must not forget, and that I owe a lot to, is Ros Lindsay – now Ros Pierce. Ros was doing her nursing training at the University of South Australia at Underdale. She was exceptionally good with Leila and did everything for her. When it came to the end and Leila had made the decision to give up all her treatment, she said she wanted to go back once more to Raukkan, and to see the Coorong. This was about a fortnight before she died. And we did just that – we took her back. Ros came with us, and she was marvellous.

You should have seen the look on Leila's face when she saw the Coorong again! We knew then what she wanted. We also took her down to Raukkan, where she met everybody and said goodbye to all those she wanted to say goodbye to. And that was a wonderful opportunity for her, because I guess many people don't get that chance to say goodbye.

Then we took her back to her house in Adelaide. She left her home for hospital that night, and she knew that it was the last time that she would ever see her house. Ros and Eddie Rigney (now deceased) took her back to Flinders Hospital and two weeks later she died there. Her doctor was absolutely wonderful, and the staff there – we can't say enough for them. And her daughters, especially Veronica – she stuck by her mother right up until the morning of the day she died. And Veronica's own sudden death not long after her mother's death stunned us all as well. Who would have thought that someone as young as her would die so soon like that?

But Leila left me something very special. She died on my birthday! So she finally had the last say with me. Yes, she died on my birthday – 15 January 1993. She was sixty-one when she died.

Another cousin of ours who was very close to Leila and me died just two weeks after Leila. That was my dear cousin Adrian Rigney (Bulla). He used to refer to himself as Reverend Bulla Harris. He was the wild man of the Coorong and he was a character. We really miss him.

Bulla was one of these guys that we thought would live on indefinitely, you know. I remember a little incident with Bulla in the days when we had a character here on TV on Channel Ten in Adelaide called Fat Cat. One day everybody was in Victoria Square. Bulla was there, and he saw Fat Cat over at the fountain. There were all these kids gathered around Fat Cat, and this one kid said to Bulla, 'How come Fat Cat don't talk?' – because he never talked on the show.

And Bulla said to him, 'Haven't you ever seen Fat Cat talk?'

And this kid said, 'No.'

So Bulla said, 'Well you'll hear him now!' And he went straight over to Fat Cat and pushed him into the fountain!

Well, Fat Cat got out of the water and said to Bulla, 'You stupid so-and-so bastard!'

And then Bulla says, 'There! Did you hear Fat Cat swear?'

So that's the sort of thing Bulla used to do. But when Leila died it broke poor old Bulla's heart, and two weeks later, Bulla ended up dying on the steps of Parliament House, on North Terrace. He had gone to sleep with Donny Smith and some others, and in the early hours of the morning Donny went to wake him and discovered that Bulla had died in the night.

Bulla was an avid Norwood barracker, and when he died he went with the team colours, blue and red. His kids put the colours on him, and he would have been so proud of them if he could have seen them.

But, as I said, Leila was very sorely missed by Bulla, and by us all. I miss Leila's wisdom; and I miss her being here – she was always there for us. I guess when she left, though, she left something with me too. She left me some wisdom, and she left me some teaching. And she gave me something of her strength and knowledge. You see, she told me of the women's sacred meanings of Hindmarsh Island. And that gave rise to another interesting chapter in my life.

Chapter 13

The Hindmarsh Island Bridge Affair

Oh, boy! That's the only way I could start off this chapter. Hindmarsh Island has become the centre of a bitter controversy that resulted in the calling of a Royal Commission by the Brown government in South Australia, and the calling of a Federal Inquiry by the then Minister of Aboriginal Affairs, Senator Robert Tickner. This all came up after Tickner halted the construction of a bridge connecting Hindmarsh Island to the mainlaind, on the grounds that the waters of that area were sacred to Ngarrindjeri women.

Hindmarsh Island is a beautiful little island down by the Murray Mouth end of the Coorong, or Kurrangk, as I prefer to call it. It is so pretty, so peaceful and so beautiful. When you stand on that little island and look out, the beautiful scenery is all the way around. In various spots on the island you can look towards the Murray Mouth, and you can look all the way up towards the Kurrangk. You can also look back towards the marina and Goolwa, or you can look across to Mundoo Island, which is known as the 'island of the dead' because that's where the dead were smoked in the tea-trees.

The whole affair began when Tom and Wendy Chapman proposed the building of a bridge from Goolwa across to Hindmarsh Island to help with transport across to their marina development there. They felt it would be far easier and quicker for cars, boats and carriers to go over on a bridge rather than on the ferry.

Up until the early 1990s, little was known or said about

Hindmarsh Island, particularly in the media. Then we discovered that the Bannon government had given the go-ahead to build the bridge. Now, when the issue came up we, the Ngarrindjeri people, tried to say, 'No! You cannot go ahead and build the bridge. There are Aboriginal bones buried on that place, so therefore you cannot build.' You see, on that island there are the graves of many Aboriginal people who died and were buried there many years ago.

Eventually, in 1993, the Environment, Resources and Development Committee of State Parliament recommended unanimously against the building of the bridge. This was on the recommendations of Ngarrindjeri people in the Lower Murray Aboriginal Heritage Committee. But by December of that year there was a new Liberal government in power in South Australia. They set up an inquiry by a lawyer, Sam Jacobs, who advised them to go ahead with the bridge.

And that's when we felt we had to reveal the fact that the waters around Hindmarsh Island are sacred to Ngarrindjeri people. It has its meaning in the women's business, and that cannot be spoken of in detail because it's strictly confidential. It's sacred to the Ngarrindjeri women and can only be spoken among Ngarrindjeri women.

After we went public, Senator Tickner halted the building of the bridge in May 1994, and asked Professor Cheryl Saunders to prepare a report on the whole issue. In that report, Professor Saunders confirmed that 'Hindmarsh and Mundoo Islands, the waters of the Goolwa channel, Lake Alexandrina and the Murray Mouth' had an important place 'within the Aboriginal tradition of Ngarrindjeri women which is crucial for the reproduction of the Ngarrindjeri people and of the cosmos which supports their existence'.

Attached to Saunders' report was a sealed envelope containing confidential anthropological detail on the women's business, which could only be read by women. It was prepared by Dr Deane Fergie, who was provided with information by the Ngarrindjeri elder, Dr Doreen Kartinyeri. Doreen had been elected as a spokesperson for the women at a meeting held amongst the Ngarrindjeri women at Graham's Castle in Goolwa. So, on the basis of the Saunders report, in July 1994 Tickner decided to ban the building of the bridge.

Now a small group of Ngarrindjeri women, who have become known as the 'dissident women', claimed they knew nothing of the women's business. They were contacted by the federal Liberal MP Ian McLachlan, who then claimed in parliament that the Ngarrindjeri women's business was a 'fabrication'. Now, those women who knew nothing of the business could have approached the other Ngarrindjeri women who knew and asked, 'What is this women's business?' They would have been told of the women's business, and it could have been explained, but unfortunately things got out of hand, and the media made a big issue of the whole affair.

The building of the bridge was on hold for a good while, and a Royal Commission was set up by the Brown government in South Australia to look into the so-called fabrication of the women's business associated with Hindmarsh Island. The Commission itself, I believe, turned into a gossip affair – not the Hindmarsh Island affair. It was unbalanced because, apart from myself, the only Ngarrindjeri women to come forward and give evidence were the dissident women. So it ended up with the dissident women telling the media things that we never ever spoke about in the Aboriginal community.

It is really heartbreaking to think what has happened. Throughout the Commission, the government pushed these women, and they made it look as if the government was right. They went ahead and did what they wanted so that the bridge could be built. And yet one of the dissident women, in an interview with her local paper, said she didn't want the bridge built.

The bridge exists now, but we, the Ngarrindjeri women, aren't happy about that. The Hindmarsh Island affair has made history across Australia. It's the first and only time that the spiritual aspect of an Aboriginal culture has been questioned. Someone in the Federal Parliament – that's McLachlan – began the story by saying that it was fabricated – but it's not fabricated. It's cultural in every aspect.

Little Hindmarsh Island has been written into the history books. The controversy over the bridge building, and the associated questioning of Aboriginal cultural history and background, is now known Australia-wide, and from here on the validity of Aboriginal culture and beliefs can be questioned elsewhere because of it. Katrina Power, a descendant of the Narungga-Kaurna people who was against the building of the bridge, asked the crowd at a protest rally whether we should now be asking if Mother Mary really was a virgin when she married Joseph. Questions just like that one are being asked about Aboriginal spiritual beliefs as a result of that Royal Commission's findings.

But on 21 August 2001, the Federal Court judge Justice von Doussa handed down his findings of the twenty-million-dollar compensation case brought to the courts by Tom and Wendy Chapman. During the process Justice von Doussa had gone thorugh all the material on the Royal Commission into the Hindmarsh Island affair. And in so doing, he came up with the finding that, 'I am not satisfied that the restricted women's knowledge was fabricated or that it was not part of genuine Aboriginal tradition'.

It's been a long-drawn-out process and a lot of hurts have been brought out with it, and a healing process needs to start now among the women. The Ngarrindjeri women are prepared to forget our pride and open our hearts to the dissident women, because we were never brought up to hate. We were brought up to love our fellow men and women, and if this has all been whiteman's doings then we have certainly fallen prey to his touches. When we fight with our own sisters, and particularly with women who we've grown up to love and look up to, it's a very sad thing.

So the Hindmarsh Island affair has drawn us out into the spotlight. There's been some hideous goings on, but at the same time there's been lots of good support from people who were against the Royal Commission – there's been heaps of support for us. The State Minister Dr Armitage was forced to conduct a community survey to see what support there was among the local Aboriginal people for the calling of the Royal Commission into the affair. Eighty-five per cent were against the Commission being held, but their opinions were pushed to one side and were never respected. Instead the government adhered to the opinions of just the fifteen per cent of people who wanted the Commission to go ahead. So you can see what the government was after. They wanted the bridge to go ahead, and they simply did not want to acknowledge the Ngarrindjeri women's business or any cultural aspects of the Ngarrindjeri people. It's money that speaks across all languages!

And it's not true when they claim that women's business doesn't exist there today. The fact is that even in this day and age it does exist, and the spirits are still there on Hindmarsh Island. As long as those bones remain in the earth on Hindmarsh Island, the spirits still walk that island. You cannot take away the fact that the Ngarrindjeri women's business did take place on Hindmarsh Island. Therefore we had to fight to try to keep that island free of towers of cement and whatever else whiteman's progress would turn it into. The bridge connecting Hindmarsh Island to the mainland has changed our culture. If we don't fight it, where will it stop? Next it will be the rest of the Kurrangk, and Ngarrindjeri culture will be wiped out. And like the old saying went years ago, 'Whiteman would prevail. In the end whiteman will see the destruction of Aboriginal culture, and we'll be left with nought.' There will be nothing left for my grandchildren or for yours.

*

Now as I mentioned earlier, my older sister Leila was a very wise woman, and when she passed on she left some of her knowledge with me. Leila was a very sick woman, and when she knew she could not go on living any more, she asked my permission to die. I did not want to give it, but she begged me, so what else could I do but say yes? I couldn't see her suffering like she was. When we knew that it was time for her to go, and she was giving up her treatment, we sat and we talked. In fact, we got talking about a whole range of things, from Raukkan right down to Adelaide. We talked about Mum and about the family, and Grandmother and about the land at Glanville and our Kaurna heritage. Then she said to me, 'Do you know anything about Hindmarsh Island?'

I said, 'No, I don't.'

She said, 'Well Mum told me, and she got it from her mother.'

And I said, 'Well how come Mum told you and didn't tell me?'

She said, 'Well, because your lifestyle was a lot different to mine – my lifestyle was on the more serious side of things.'

She was referring to the cultural side of things. You see, Leila never drank or smoked, but I did, so her closeness to the culture was much more appreciated by my mother than mine. Mum knew I was drinking and carrying on like I was, and she thought I certainly wasn't a good person to tell any of the sacred cultural stuff to.

But Leila knew before she died that it was the right time to mention things. She saw that I had been so many years off the drink, and I was capable of being told the women's business. So she told me, and I was quite amazed – I was quite shocked.

It really opened my eyes. I didn't know any culture like that existed for our Ngarrindjeri women, but it does! And in a way I reckon it's great. If only our younger Ngarrindjeri women could learn of it, it might help them – it might do something for them. It won't, however, unless they're prepared to give up some of their present life, and the way they're living life today. I believe you've got to combine Aboriginal culture with what you're doing – you've got to have the strength to draw on that Aboriginal culture. But while you're living the wild way and doing all these foolish things, you're certainly not going to be able to give to your culture. So you have to make a decision.

I was pleased – I was really glad that Leila told me about the women's business. But her girls said to me, 'Why didn't Mum tell us?'

And I said, 'Because Mum saw how you fellas go on. Your lifestyle is enough to tell an elder that they can't tell you anything, because they know that you'd blabbermouth. You might say you won't do it. But that's not telling her that you're not going to do it, because she knows you better.'

You see, sometimes our parents know us better than we know ourselves.

Leila's girls were happy with that, and I said to them, 'When the time's right, I'll sit you all down and tell you.'

So Leila's wisdom in telling me what she did, and the other talks that we had, made me feel really good after she went. Because she didn't leave me without anything – she left me with a lot of things. Sometimes I hear her in my bedroom, walking around. You get to know that feeling between the different spirits that come round, and I just say, 'Leila, I'm all right. You can go, I'm all right.' And I hear the footsteps walk out the door, and I go sound asleep.

The other night there was footsteps. They were shuffling around in the passage, and I sang out, 'Whoever you are, I'm all right. Go away, go on!' And the footsteps stopped and I went sound asleep. Jim hears them quite often too when I'm not there or even if I'm home. He'll hear them. He knows that I hear them from my bedroom, but I don't sing out to him, 'Did you hear footsteps?'

But he says to me, 'How come they don't frighten you?'

Even my best girlfriend Tootie – that's Gloria Sparrow's sister – I feel her presence sometimes. That Tootie used to spend almost every weekend at my place, but one week she became extremely ill and collapsed at home and never recovered. I was waiting for her to come, and she was taking a long time, so I thought, I'd better go and see where she is. Then Gloria came and told me she'd been rushed to the Queen Elizabeth Hospital. So then we went up there to see her, because she and I were very close, but she died. But even today I still expect her to pop her head round the door one night and say, 'Hi!' – just as she used to do. So the footsteps don't frighten me, but I know the spirits are there.

And I think with all this stuff that has been going on with Hindmarsh Island, there's now a lot more spirits with us – they're becoming active. Auntie Maggie Jacobs could tell you about the spirits she's been feeling of late, and the spirits that I've been feeling are the spirits that other people have been feeling. Now the funny thing is, somebody warned one day that when this Hindmarsh Island thing started, the spirits were going to rise up. It was said years ago down along Raukkan that if Ngarrindjeri people didn't pull together, the spirits would rise and there would be trouble. Well look at what's happening today – we've got lots of trouble now. Heaps of trouble.

I think it's time some people started to take notice of what's happening with our spirits, and looking at what's happening to us as a people. We need to look at our health and look at our children. What have we got to offer our children if we are going to be fighting among ourselves? We've got nothing to offer them. And so we must unite, we must come together as the big family we were before all this started. We mustn't allow whiteman's greed to come in and separate us. If we allow that to happen, then we don't deserve to be a nation. Our Ngarrindjeri nation was a proud nation once – because of the things that our people did and achieved in the past. They were a wonderful nation. Self-educated, self-motivators, home-makers, carpenters, everything – you name it. These people were talented, and we're highly intelligent people, so why are we allowing this to happen to us? Is it the manipulation of whiteman's greed?

Greed and money – that's what it is. I mean, you go back to the old blackfella's way of living. He was never greedy – he shared. And among all that sharing there was a lot of love. Today there's a lot of greed, and a lot of anger and nastiness is going on because of that greed. They're allowing greed to overpower them, you know. They're allowing money to take over. It's the whitefellas who are pushing the blackfellas, and manipulating them into denying their culture. But money won't buy them their pride back as a people, that's for sure. You know, when that culture is gone, they're going to have nothing.

The things that have been said by some of the dissident women have to be sorted out and dealt with. We've got to say to these women, 'You know, you must come and sit down and we must talk about all this. We can't allow this fighting to go on. You've got to tell us your side of it. But don't let the whitefellas come in and manipulate you and use you as a pawn in their games against us!' Because that's what we've been – pawns in a bigger game of greed and power.

I don't think these people realise the extent of the damage that will be caused to the Ngarrindjeri culture now that the bridge is built. Because it's not the bridge itself that will cause the damage, but the fact that it crosses the water. It's the water around that island that is sacred. And it is also the things that happened on the island itself – the Ngarrindjeri women's business. What more can I say about such things? I mean, you don't go and question the Pitjantjatjara women up north about their women's business. They'd clobber you. The fact that our women's business is no longer being performed isn't our doing, but it once happened and will continue to happen – and that's why that island is sacred. That top part of the island is sacred, because of the same things that take place with the Pitjantjatjara women's business today. And so why are we being questioned?

It just doesn't make common sense to hold a Royal Commission to question the validity of that business, just because somebody said, 'Oh, it's a fabrication.' They don't know that! The dissident women might not have known the business, but they can't say that it never happened. That's the point that we tried to get across to the old Commissioner, Iris Stevens.

You think people would learn after they've destroyed the Murray Mouth – that's what whiteman did! They dug that mouth section out and moved it a bit to the left, and moving it that way has changed the whole flow of the Kurrangk, which is wrong. Now you've got boats that can go right in there to the mouth, and trucks and four-wheel drives can drive all along the beach from Goolwa to the mouth. One year there was half a dozen four-wheel drives floating around in that water – brand new four-wheel drives! The night tide came in and flooded them, and all these four-wheel drives were trapped. That's what happens when you tamper with nature. The natural flow of water down the Kurrangk has been ruined, just as it was by the erection of the barrages near Goolwa in the 1950s.

When this whole Hindmarsh Island business came up, I said that Leila died two years too soon. Had she been around, she might have been able to do something to help stop all the fighting. But then again, it probably would have destroyed her. She would have been horrified to see what's happened. Because Hindmarsh Island is the island where Dad used to go every year – he never missed the swan-egg season. He'd come back with bags and bags of swan eggs. But with that bridge in place, there'll be nothing – cement and tar will rule Hindmarsh Island.

Chapter 14

Commissions and Inquiries

The Royal Commission on the proposed Hindmarsh Island bridge began in July 1995, and was called by the Brown government to inquire:

whether the 'women's business' or any aspect of the 'women's business' was a fabrication and, if so:
a) the circumstances relating to such a fabrication;
b) the extent of the fabrication;
c) the purpose of such fabrication.

Apart from the handful of dissident women, most of us Ngarrindjeri women refused to be a part of the Royal Commission, on the grounds that we did not recognise its authority. I was one of the twenty-three women who signed a statement presented to the commissioner in the first week of the Inquiry, that began:

We are deeply offended that a Government in this day and age has the audacity to order an inquiry into our secret, sacred, spiritual beliefs. Never before have any group of people had their spiritual beliefs scrutinised in this way.

It is our responsibility as custodians of this knowledge to protect it. Not only from the men, but also from those not entitled to this knowledge. We have a duty to keep Aboriginal law in this country.

Women's business does exist, has existed since time immemorial and will continue to exist where there are Aboriginal women who are able to continue to practise their culture.

The Royal Commission ended, with the last witness being heard, in November 1995. I continued to boycott the Commission by refusing to give evidence, even though I was called to. But some of the things that were being said by the dissident women, and some of the things being said by the lawyers, worried me. Then, during the last week of the inquiry, I changed my mind and decided to go before the Commissioner. Partly I felt that I needed to support those who had given evidence before me, even though they were very unhappy about the commission – people like the Ngarrindjeri men: Henry Rankine, Tom Trevorrow and George Trevorrow – people who gave support to the existence of women's business. I felt they needed that moral support. I also felt that my mother needed that support and my sister, because when my mother's name came up in the evidence, it was implied that she was a liar. But my mother, even though she was a Christian woman, was not deterred from believing in her culture, and believing in what she had been told by the elders.

You see, back in 1967 my mother (also known as Kumi) met with a woman called Betty Fisher, and she talked to Betty about the sacredness of the waters around Hindmarsh Island. But she only told the surface of the story to Betty Fisher, who was working on a book at the time with Auntie Gladdy Elphick. Betty wasn't told too much – the secrets were kept by my mother. However, Betty recorded some information in a notebook. Who would have known, in that day and age, that the information given then would be needed in 1995? Maybe my mother saw into the future and she knew that the information she gave would one day help her Ngarrindjeri people!

Betty Fisher was called before the Royal Commission to give evidence regarding the recordings she made with my mother, Kumi, and the notes she made in her notebook. Betty no longer has those notes in her possession, but they

Myself on the Tjilbruke trail, at Warriparinga

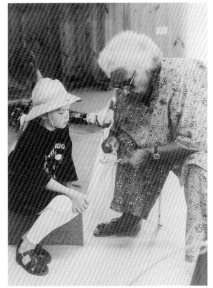

Spiritual rejuvenation at Camp Coorong, basket weaving

Still studying at 58 years of age

More public speaking by yours truly

The Hindmarsh Island ferry

Construction of the Hindmarsh Island bridge

Protest at the Hindmarsh Island bridge opening

Protest rallies against the Hindmarsh Island bridge

My respected elder Auntie Maggie Jacobs and myself

Lake Alexandrina at Raukkan

My cousins Kath Burgemeister, Cherie Watkins and myself

My grandson JJ at the fish traps
made down the Coorong

Me and my daughters
Kathleen and Margaret

A weekend on the Gale farm with Mary-Anne, myself, Auntie Maggie Jacobs, Cherie Watkins, Rob Amery and Mary-Anne's daughters Jemima and Miriam

Students doing Kaurna Studies at Tauondi College

questioned her constantly about them in the Commission. That dear old lady went in to give evidence because she thought it was the right thing to do – because she thought she should divulge the fact that Kumi had told her about there being women's business on Hindmarsh Island. She thought she might be able to put an end to what was happening between the Ngarrindjeri women. So she brought out the information on the *7.30 Report* on ABC television,

But at the Commission they tried to say that it was fabricated. In other words, they were trying to make my mother look like a liar! And that hurt us very much, my family and me. What happened over this whole affair is heart-wrenching and heartbreaking. Some days left me feeling sore, as though my body had been beaten – all because of what this Royal Commission has done to a wonderful nation, the Ngarrindjeri nation. It's ripped us apart; it's made enemies of relatives; and if the old ones were still living, can you imagine what they would have been saying and doing to us today? They probably would have got the *kanakis* (fighting clubs) out and the waddies, and flogged us with them. That would've been their way of showing us, and saying to us, 'You know we don't approve of this!'

And yet, when you look at what some people have done – they've turned our own against us. It was a sad day, that day that I received the notice calling me into the Royal Commission. They wanted me to verify that it was my mother's voice on Betty Fisher's recording. My dear mother's name had been thrown around in that Royal Commission for two or three weeks. I'd sat in there for one day, and that was enough for me – I couldn't stand to sit there any longer and hear my mother's name thrown around any more. So I decided to stay at home and to stay out of it. But at the same time it worried me that they were implying my mother was a liar.

And then one night my family and I came to grips with this whole affair about Hindmarsh Island. I made my decision. I said, 'I'm not going into the Royal Commission again. I'm not going to tell them anything.' Even though the information given to me on my sister's deathbed coincided with a lot of things that were being said at that hearing, I decided they were not going to get it. That secret stays with me.

And I had the full support of my eldest brother in my decision, which was important to me – it's vitally important that we have the elders' support. Even the dissident women have an elder that they should be coming to and adhering to – and that's Auntie Maggie Jacobs. We learnt to respect our elders when we were growing up on Raukkan. I mean, even Doreen Kartinyeri is my elder, and I respect her. Anyone older than myself – which may not seem too many – I must respect them. But we must all respect each other and love each other, because with that respect we know we can look to one another in difficult times.

But that night with my family, it was then that I made a decision not to co-operate any further with the Commission. I lay in bed that night, and for the first time since my mother's name started coming up in the Commission, I slept all night. I think it was because I had made the right decision. Before that, all I could think of was the Royal Commission – again and again, and it was coming at me from all corners of the earth. It was buzzing round and round in my head and it was making me sick. I kept thinking, what will I do? Will I go into that Commission, or won't I? It was just about driving me silly. Then, after I had made my decision, I lay down and started to drift off to sleep, and then I thought to myself, I'm at peace now. I know what my decision is. All along they'd been grabbing at straws to get evidence from the proponent women at that Commission, and I was the last straw that they could grab at. That's why they tried to drag me in, but it suddenly occurred to me that this straw here wasn't going to be used for their purposes!

But as things turned out, I still had them banging on my door and sending me 'nice' letters or ringing my phone – so it continued to worry me, and I still couldn't sleep peacefully. They still wanted the letters that Betty Fisher had written to me, and they wanted any other things that I had – even though I said, 'I'll burn them! I'll do that today, I'll burn them! I'll just keep them in my head.' Because that's what the elders did when they passed away – they didn't leave anything written down. It all went with them in their heads, because they knew they couldn't trust whiteman with their secrets. The bit of language and culture they left behind was not written down.

So during the last week of the Commission I did come forward to give evidence to the Commissioner, as a Ngarrindjeri woman. But when I was in the box, I was questioned in detail about my Kaurna heritage by the lawyers – as if that invalidated my evidence. They didn't seem to understand that many Aboriginal people have links to two different groups through their mothers and their fathers. It is common throughout much of Australia to marry someone from a different language group to your own. So on the Ngarrindjeri side, I have my grandfather Dan Wilson, my grandmother Bessie Wilson, and another grandparent Jacob Harris. They were my three Ngarrindjeri grandparents. But I had one Kaurna grandparent, Laura Glanville Harris, née Spender.

Now when you consider the one-sided evidence given at that Royal Commission, I guess you would expect Commissioner Iris Stevens to produce a report that came down on the side of the government. I mean, the government was contractually bound to construct the Hindmarsh Island bridge, and if they didn't they would be liable for a huge compensation bill from the Chapman family. We still hoped in our hearts that the Commissioner would come down on our side, but she didn't – she came down on the side of the government. So for me it was a heartbreaking outcome, especially knowing that eighty-five per cent of the Ngarrindjeri community thought the whole Commission should have been abolished. No trust was given to us by the government.

There are some incidents that occurred during this whole business that are really regrettable. Doug Milera, who has since passed on, said some things down at Victor Harbor against the women. He was interviewed by journalist Chris Kenny, who met him down there at the Appollon Motel to get it all on video. It just shows how desperate things were getting. But we, as Ngarrindjeri women, look beyond that, because we can see what was done. What we heard Doug say may have hurt us at the time, but we realise the pressure Doug was under with alcohol, and we forgave him, because we loved him.

I was up before the Royal Commission for two days and gave my information. It was very difficult for me, because I didn't have any counsel representing me. By that stage the Aboriginal Legal Service had pulled out. But because I felt that I needed to fight for our beliefs, I came forward to be questioned. You know there's a beautiful Dreaming story that goes with Hindmarsh Island, and that's *The Seven Sisters*. And there's also that wonderful relationship that our women had with the whales and the dolphins – and that's something that the Ngarrindjeri dissident women apparently did not believe. So they should have come to us and asked us and we could have told them.

I'm hoping that very soon I'll be able to reveal that knowledge to those Ngarrindjeri women. Maybe at a meeting at the Kurrangk one weekend I'll be able to give them what they really need to know and what they need to think about. Because I had that knowledge, I was able to fight for Hindmarsh Island. It's a beautiful island. I suppose you could say it's impregnated with a wonderful Aboriginal spirituality.

The sun has finally set on Hindmarsh Island, and the Ngarrindjeri women have been vindicated with their win in the Federal Court. This is the beginning of the rebirth of Ngarrindjeri culture. The whales will return to Victor Harbor. In fact, they are already coming back, because the whole history of the women's business revolves around Hindmarsh Island, Victor Harbor, Port Elliot, and in particular around the whales coming back. You see, the whales were the life-givers to the women.

We have decided never to cross the new 'suicide bridge'. It has caused so much ill-feeling that maybe one day nature in its own way may bring the bridge down. Who knows? For some time now it has been the hope of the Ngarrindjeri people that the government fully support us with a ferry at another crossing to the island, so that we can carry on with our cultural activities. After the handing down of the von Doussa findings we hope the government now understands our feelings about crossing those cultural waters via the bridge.

The Royal Commission and the subsequent Federal Court decision was a lesson to all of us Ngarrindjeri women. It taught us a lot. It taught us to be strong and to never give up our beliefs and our culture, and to never give up our Aboriginality. In reference to the dissident women, they have denied any knowledge of their culture that relates to women – so they have nothing left of their culture, and I think that's very sad.

One of the key dissident women, Dulcie Wilson, wrote a letter to the *Adelaide Review*, and she spoke of Christ dying on the cross and the hurt that he must have felt for his fellow Christians. I wonder if Dulcie knows of the hurt that she caused her people. Why couldn't she come to her own Ngarrindjeri women?

For those women to say that they didn't even know where Hindmarsh Island was is shameful. They should be ashamed to call themselves Ngarrindjeri, they are from Raukkan. So it's no wonder they weren't told any secrets about it. The old women were very careful about who they told their secrets to.

And Sue Lawrie was the one who first contacted the dissident women for Ian McLachlan. She's done her father a disservice – she's the daughter of Mack Lawrie, who grew up on Raukkan with us Ngarrindjeri people. She's the grand-daughter of old W.T. Lawrie, who was a lovely old person really. So this Commission was very revealing.

The Royal Commission report itself states that the dissident women, some of whom lived completely Western lives, didn't know anything of the women's business. So how does that prove that it was a fabrication? You can't say it's a fabrication just because those women said they didn't know anything about it. That doesn't mean that it doesn't exist. Iris Stevens, the Royal Commissioner, doesn't know anything about Aboriginal culture, so I believe she should never have been given the job.

Look at the Brown government – and look at Brown himself. Look at what he said. When the decision was handed down from the Commission, he said it would be 'a landmark in Aboriginal history that this fabrication had taken place'. And I mean how could he call it a fabrication? He didn't know, and neither did McLachlan. He only went on what the dissident women told him. McLachlan's staff were the ones who got hold of the secret envelope attached to Deane Fergie's report, and copied them. He eventually had to resign from the front bench for that.

From my side of the bridge, there will never be and there never was fabrication of the women's business on Hindmarsh Island. Because if you look at the history, the whales *are* coming back, and they are going to continue to come back. And maybe the women's business will continue one day on Hindmarsh Island, who knows? That's only for us to know, and for those who are inquisitive enough to find out.

Cultural activities don't have to come back in the exact same form as they occurred years ago. All cultures change. Whiteman has made sure of that! But the important thing is that the women's business does come back one day, and we know that we've got the young women here who we can teach. For that to return would give us a sense of self-respect and a sense of belonging – of being Aboriginal again, you know. And that's what we basically need to get back – knowing our Aboriginality, and knowing who we are and where we came from – that's all part of our culture.

As I said before, we were all taught to love, not to hate. And on the strength of that love, we Ngarrindjeri women have had to try and get through the hard times we've had. We've had to face a whole community out there, both black and white, but mainly white, who were up in arms about the amount of money that was spent on the Royal Commission. The two million dollars it cost was out of taxpayers' money.

But having the final report say that the women's business was a fabrication – knowing how much we thought of our culture, and how much we loved it – well, it really hurt. It was hard to listen to such a result. When I hear these things, it makes me wonder if I'm doing the right thing in maintaining my belief in women's business. But because I know my source and where it came from, which was a true and good source, I need not worry. Knowing the truth within my heart, I feel good about it.

Although the results of the Royal Commission left us feeling downhearted and drained, we knew we had to keep fighting. Its results just made us more determined. So in 1996 we started up a new fight through Tickner's Federal Inquiry. We hoped that this Inquiry would be less biased in its terms of reference, and more sympathetic towards Aboriginal beliefs and culture. The calling of the Federal Inquiry enabled us to give some of the information required to prove our beliefs. We thought this would help people see that the women's business was *not* a fabrication.

The Inquiry was run by Federal Court Judge Jane Mathews, who was appointed by the Labor government before they lost the Federal election in 1996. Auntie Maggie Jacobs and a few of us other Ngarrindjeri women who had knowledge of the women's business decided to co-operate with the Federal Inquiry into the Hindmarsh Island bridge affair. It was very interesting to hear what that old lady, Auntie Maggie, had to say in the Inquiry. I respect her to the utmost, and I know that what she gave would have been a real eye-opener to the dissident women and to McLachlan. The Federal Inquiry went into things that Iris Stevens never dreamed of.

But in September 1996 I was shocked to hear that a High Court of Australia challenge by the dissident women had succeeded in having the decision of Justice Mathews made invalid. We heard that before the report was even tabled in parliament by the new Federal Minister for Aboriginal Affairs, Mr John Herron – and the Inquiry had cost over a million dollars to hold! The High Court judged that it was unconstitutional to have a federal judge running the Inquiry. So suddenly we didn't know where we stood.

Tom and George Trevorrow took Justice Mathews down to the Kurrangk and showed her the land that is so important to our people. And I had to tell my story to her. I felt sad that I had to reveal some of what I know, but for the sake of Ngarrindjeri women it was told with much love, much emotion, and much feeling. Emotionally it was a very traumatic time for me, because when you're bound by confidentiality to someone who is no longer living and you break that promise, then you wonder what's going to happen to you.

See, that's not how things were passed on to others in traditional times. Our ways had to change, because the government didn't want us to keep our culture and beliefs; they wanted us to assimilate. That's why they took so many children from their mothers and put them in white homes. So when women's knowledge was passed on to others, in later years, it was passed on to the wisest one in the family. So when it was time, it was handed down to the wisest woman in your family – which I think is a wonderful way!

At the Federal Inquiry, we were represented by our own female lawyer, Pam Ditton, and she had an anthropologist, Dr Diane Bell, assisting her. We hoped our lawyer could establish the fact that women's business did happen on Hindmarsh Island without having to reveal too much about what actually happened. Pam Ditton thought we might be able to get away without revealing too many details – mainly for my sake, because Leila told me in confidence. Doreen and I were the main two who knew. The others didn't know – but, as I said before, Auntie Maggie knows some too. It's funny, because I'd never spoken to Auntie Maggie, and I'd never spoken to Doreen about it before all this, and what those two say is what Leila told me. Each has a lot of similarity to the other.

Where Doreen got her information from I don't know. She says Auntie Rosie gave it to her, and I believe Auntie Rosie could have told her. But even if she got it from somebody else, or even from the museum – if they had it (but they don't) – as an historian, I believe that she has a right to know. Some men at the museum said they didn't think that women's business existed, and said that even though women's business did exist elsewhere, it didn't exist amongst Ngarrindjeri women. But, being white males, they wouldn't know what happened anyway.

None of the dissident women who gave evidence at the Royal Commission were called before the Federal Inquiry, and the media were not allowed to witness the hearing this time either – it was all held in private. That's why not much was reported in the papers or on the TV. Michael Abbott QC was amongst it all, though. It was him who took the dissident women's challenge to the High Court regarding Jane Mathews's appointment. You can't help but feel for him. I'm not sure how much he knows of Aboriginal culture. I thought his line of questioning to me in the Royal Commission was puzzling. If he was going to go in there and question Ngarrindjeri people about cultural business, then he should have had some knowledge of Aboriginal culture. The comical part came when he mentioned Margaret Jacobs, and all I could hear in the background was, 'Poor old Maggie, poor old Maggie Jacobs.' Of course it was Auntie Maggie in the gallery, calling out from the back. Abbott had this grin on his face and he didn't know which way to look. Auntie Maggie was getting to him by the end of the day.

Michael Abbott implied at one stage that my mother, my sister Leila and I were making things up. I wonder now what he thinks of the von Doussa decision in the Federal Court.

People from both side of this whole affair have been left hurt. One thing is for sure: there is a real need for reconciliation, not just within the Ngarrindjeri nation, but also between Aboriginal people and whites. There is a great need for love and forgiveness all round.

Chapter 15

The Stolen Generation

When I think of the stolen generation, it makes me sad to think of all those kids who were taken away from their families and their culture. Sometimes I think some of them were put in homes and sent to schools where they were taught to speak English so that they wouldn't have time to think about their own culture. But the government was very wrong in taking those children away. English was the only thing they ever learnt in schools, so when they got older they weren't able to relate back to their people and culture. And if they did return to get to know their Aboriginal family and culture, they were still overcome with many problems.

We've got kids who have suicided because they can't cope in a mixed world. They just can't cope with the transition of being brought up with a white family, and then suddenly being introduced to a world of Aboriginal culture. They get totally lost. They can't seem to pick up the pieces when they finally meet their relatives and are reunited with their mothers and fathers – it sort of throws them. It's very difficult for them to try and close that gap when they haven't seen their family for years.

These stolen children often have the added burden of trying to understand why they were taken away. Sometimes they prefer to believe the government departments rather than believe what their own people tell them. You see, I have two nephews who were taken away as children from Raukkan, and I had that fight with one of my nephews when I found him. He solely and wholly believed that his mother neglected him. But I said, 'No! You are wrong. She didn't neglect you!'

Their mother was my cousin. Actually my mother and her mother were sisters, and we were brought up like sisters, because her mother died when she was young. Her name was Caroline Gollan. Her two boys were taken away when one was two years old and the other one was just a baby of three weeks.

She was a single mother, you see, and there was no work on the mission. And they didn't have single parent benefits or pensions in those days that women could live on. They told her she had to go and find employment and that they would foster her children out until such a time came that she could provide for them. So she did. She signed the foster papers. I was there when both children were taken away – their names were Mel and Peter.

Since that time my cousin had always gone into the Protection Board to ask if she could see her sons. And they would arrange for the foster-mother to bring one of the boys to the Protection Board or out to Sussex Street in North Adelaide. At the time, it didn't hit home to either of us how quick one of the foster-mothers was to bring the boy over to the women's home to visit us. We didn't find out until a couple of years later that the foster woman's sister lived just around the corner.

A few years later, when my cousin was in employment, she asked for her two boys to be returned. She went into the Protection Board and inquired about getting them back. But they said, 'Oh, you'll have to wait.' The excuse was that the boys were away on holidays. But these were only excuses. Other times the Protection Board would say they couldn't locate them, or they'd say that as soon as they did locate them they would get in touch and get the boys back to her.

When my cousin got married and had her other two children, she said 'Well, we'll get these boys back now.' Her husband knew all about the boys when they got married. So she went down to what was then Aboriginal Affairs.

She said to them, 'I want to come and get my two sons.'

But they just told her, 'Do you remember in such and such a year when we went down to Raukkan to pick the boys up, and you signed the papers?'

She said, 'Yeah, I remember – they were foster papers. I agreed to have my sons fostered while I was working.'

But they replied, 'No. You had them adopted. You signed adoption papers.'

Now, my cousin isn't the only woman who I've heard of having that same experience. I've heard of lots of mums who had the same thing happen. They were basically tricked, because nobody read them the fine print on the 'foster' papers.

Just before my cousin died, I promised her that I'd find these two boys. I said to her, 'I'll find them.' I hadn't hunted for them for twenty-nine years while their mother was still alive. But when she died I thought I'd find these two boys, so a couple of years later I started the hunt.

I started my hunt at Link-up. When I gave them the names of Mel and Peter Gollan, they said, 'No, we only have one boy named Peter, and his name is now Andrew Brown.'

I thought to myself, it might be the boy I'm looking for. I don't know.

In the meantime, I thought that I'd try and find his brother, Mel, because I knew the adopted name of that boy was Train. There were only three numbers in the phone book under that name, so I rang each one. Eventually I got on to the right one. An old lady answered, and I explained to her what I was after. And she said to me, 'Look, I can tell you where to find him.' But she said to me, 'No one's bothered all these years.'

But I know that when their mother was alive she did try to find them. By the time she did find out where they were, the department told her that they were adopted out. You had no visiting rights once they were adopted. They just shoved pieces of paper under the women's noses in those days and said, 'Sign!' But what they were signing weren't the foster papers they thought they were signing. So the kids were automatically taken and couldn't be easily found. When she did start looking for them, she just didn't know where to look.

So I said to this old woman, 'Give me the address and the phone number of where I might contact Mel.'

She said, 'Ring up the hotel at Wallaroo. He's a fisherman. He comes in some days and picks up messages from the hotel.'

So I rang the hotel on the Monday and left my number. On the following Friday the phone rang at my work. When I picked up the receiver it went beep, beep, beep. And I thought, who's this ringing me long distance? And it was this boy.

He said, 'Hello. Veronica Brodie?' Then he said, 'This is Mel.'

And I thought, oh, hell. What am I goin' to say? I was stuck for words.

He said, 'You want to see me?'

I said, 'Yes. I'm your mother's cousin, but we were brought up like sisters. Your grandmother and my mother were sisters.' So I said to him, 'I've been trying to find you.'

He said, 'Where's my mother now?'

I said, 'Your mother died.'

There was silence for a while, and then he said, 'I'll come down to Adelaide to see you.'

Well, he came down to Adelaide pretty quickly, because he was here by the Sunday. And I talked for hours to this boy when he arrived, and you should have heard him! He said, 'I hate my adoptive parents.'

I said, 'Why?'

Now, normally when you bury people you bury them with respect, but not Mel. He said, 'That old bitch. I stood there and laughed at her graveside when they lowered her down.'

And I looked at him and I said, 'Mel, what has happened to you?'

He said, 'You know, I saw money change hands for my adoption.' He said, 'I got hold of my birth certificate and my father's and mother's names are both changed on it. And they changed the place of my birth to draw me away from finding my parents.'

I said, 'Well, look. You're not with them any more. How about you try and sort out your Aboriginality? Come down and visit us as many times as you like and we can talk and tell you about your mother and father.'

'OK,' he said.

And then I told him, 'You have a brother that we have to find, so we can fit the family back together.'

Now those two boys also have a half-brother and a half-sister – the step sister's just beautiful. She was the head of the Aboriginal and Torres Strait Islander section at Telstra. I said to Mel, 'Look, come and meet your sister.'

So he did, and when he finally met her he said, 'Gee, I've got a lovely sister.'

I said, 'Well, all we have to do now is find your brother Peter, and fit him into the family picture.' But the trouble was I wasn't quite sure where to start.

We kept in touch with Mel, but unfortunately he hit the drink pretty heavy because he was finding it difficult to fit into two worlds – the Aboriginal world and the white world. But he also had other problems. I think some things happened to him during those years he was in adoptive care. What, I don't know, because he never talked about it. He just says they were bastards. He says he hasn't hated anyone so much in all his life.

So eventually it came time for me to start looking for the other brother, Peter. So again I went into the Link-up office here in Adelaide, in Grenfell Street. I always call it the menagerie, because it's a big glass building. So I kept on Link-up's back about searching for this missing brother.

I said to them, 'Could I have a look at the register?' and they said, 'No.' So I reminded them that his name was Peter Gollan, and asked them if they could look it up.

So they looked it up and they said, 'We've got an Andrew Brown here. His name was originally Peter Gollan.'

And I said, 'Well, he must be the one.'

The year was 1950 or some time around then when he was taken. So I said, 'Can you contact him? Or can you give me a number that I can contact him by?'

And they said, 'No. We'll contact him and then get in touch with you.' Which they did, but it took them about four or five months. Finally they contacted me one day to say that this Andrew (or Peter) lives in Katoomba in New South Wales. He grew up there, because as soon as the Aborigines Protection Board informed the adoptive parents that this mother was looking for her children, they sold up shop here in Adelaide and moved to Katoomba.

So when I heard from Link-up that they had moved all the way over there, I said, 'Do you know if he wants to contact any of his family?' They said he didn't, so I asked if they would at least let me talk to his adoptive mother. They were a bit dubious about this idea, but they did end up giving me her number.

So I rang this adoptive mother to talk to her, and she said, 'Oh, Andrew. What relation are you?'

And I said, 'Putting it the Aboriginal way, I'm his mother's sister.'

I let her know that Andrew had family back here in Adelaide and that we would like him to meet them.

She eventually said, 'Well, I can let Andrew speak to you. I'll just go and call him.' But I could sense from her voice that she was very frightened of what she thought was going to happen.

So Andrew came to the phone, and he said, 'Look, what's this all about?'

'Well, Andrew,' I said, 'your mother was my sister. I have recently found your brother and now I'm looking for you. I would like you to come to Adelaide to meet us.'

But he said, 'What? I was bloody neglected.'

I said, 'Hold on, hold on. That was what the Protection Board told your adoptive mother. But it's not what I saw and know about.'

So I tried to explain to him that he was well looked after by his mother, but she couldn't keep him because she was a single mum. But right or wrong, he wouldn't have it. He said, 'No. I don't want to meet anybody.'

So I said, 'That's all right – fine. But before you go you can have my telephone number.' I said, 'When you feel like ringing me, ring. I'll be happy to talk to you.'

But to my surprise, in the next couple of weeks I got a phone call from his adoptive mother. I asked her, 'Has Andrew cooled down?' But what really worried me was his attitude, and the fact that he was being so brash with his statements about being neglected. He seemed to have an attitude problem against Aboriginal people.

She said, 'Well look, maybe I can send some photos over.'

I said, 'Yeah, you can.' But then I thought I'd just ask this question out of the blue, so I said, 'Did you know Andrew had a natural brother?'

'Oh yes,' she said.

I immediately responded, 'How did you know?'

She said, 'Oh, they used to play together as little boys down at Christies Beach.'

To which I said, 'You mean to tell me you knew the adoptive mother of the other brother, and you met at Christies Beach and let the two boys play together, knowing they were brothers, and you never told them?'

'Oh yes,' she said. 'We just didn't think it was necessary to tell them.' So I told her how disappointed I felt in hearing this.

She disgusted me to think that she treated the boys like this. I was furious, and I said to her, 'Oh look, I'll call you another time.' And I hung up on her.

In the meantime, I was trying to help this other boy Mel, and to get him to meet some of his relations – his father's relations. Anyhow, one day we got talking, and I said, 'Where did you live?'

He said, 'I lived seven kilometres out of Cowell on the west coast.'

'Well,' I said to him in dismay, 'Would you like to know where your mother is buried?'

He said, 'Where?'

And I told him, 'She's in the Cowell cemetery!'

'What?'

I said, 'Mel, you must've passed your mother in Cowell I don't know how many times before she passed away, and you didn't even know it was her. Your adoptive parents must have recognised your mother.'

But you see, they wouldn't say anything. They chose to keep it from him, even though he grew up in the same area. So he didn't know that his mother was around there all that time.

Getting back to the other brother, it would have been three or four months since my conversation with the woman who adopted Andrew, when finally Link-up got back in touch with me. This time they said that Andrew was looking to come over to Adelaide. I thought, God, what are we going to do here? But fortunately his half-sister had been thinking and working very hard towards this possible reunion – she's a lovely girl, Rebecca – and she said, 'Aunt, you've got to bring them to my place.'

I said, 'Yes. But we've got to meet this boy first. We don't know what we're coming up against.'

So suddenly this idea came to me. See, there was this young boy, Jonathon Brown – he's a wonderful Aboriginal artist. He even painted a jacket for Mick Jagger and presented it to him at his concert in Melbourne. Jonathon Brown turned out to be Andrew's adopted brother. I didn't know this at the time, but when I heard the name Brown, I thought, I wonder if this Jonathon knows anything about Andrew? It was just an idea off the top of my head. So I eventually discovered that they were adopted brothers and that Jonathon had left Katoomba to go back to Yalata to find his people. And I thought, I wonder what Jonathon's attitude is? I wonder how he got on when he returned to his people? If he's got on all right, I wonder if he could talk to Andrew? You see, these boys were brought up as brothers, not knowing they had brothers outside.

So I decided to ring Yalata. I don't know how many times I tried to ring to try and get hold of Jonathon. He was always out. Anyhow, before I went to bed one night, just before midnight, I tried ringing again, and this time he answered the phone. So I told him who I was and what I wanted. He said to me, 'Well, Auntie, all I can do is ring him and talk to him.' So he rang Andrew for me and spoke to him.

I told my oldest daughter about me ringing Jonathon, and she said to me, 'Mum, has it ever occurred to you that some of these kids are brought up white?'

I said, 'But how can they be brought up white with such dark skins?'

Then she said, 'Think about it.'

So I started to think, and I started to realise what had happened. You see, Andrew couldn't see beyond his nose. He was white as far as he was concerned. All he'd seen around him was white people – not Aboriginal. He had nothing to do with Aboriginal people except for Jonathon. It didn't sink into him about the way he'd been brought up. The word 'Aboriginal' was never mentioned.

It was only then that it occurred to me what we were actually dealing with. So I said to Rebecca, 'Well, when he comes over, what will we do?' We decided then to get Link-up to help us.

Link-up eventually said, 'He's coming over on the bus.'

And I said, 'Well, why don't we let the two brothers meet each other first? Then we'll meet them after.'

So when Andrew arrived, we let Mel meet him first and then we got there ten minutes later. And it was the most emotional scene that I have ever come across – two brothers were hangin' onto one another and bawlin' their eyes out!

When Mel saw Andrew, he immediately remembered this little boy that he had played with at Christies Beach. Yeah, it was an incredible thing that he remembered the face of this little boy he played with. You see, Mel was the older of the two.

Andrew eventually went to Adelaide Uni and TAFE – he did Aboriginal Studies to understand more about his Aboriginality; he's working on his culture and history. He's lovely to talk to. His adoptive mother came over and she brought photos of the two boys playing at Christies Beach together. She also bawled her eyes out.

She said, 'I'm sorry I did this to your people.'

But I said, 'You didn't do it to me – you done it to them!'

Since then Andrew, through Freedom of Information, went to Births, Deaths and Marriages, and demanded they give him his birth certificate. And when he got it he discovered his mother and father's names were changed – as well as his own name. They also changed his birth date. He said, 'Look at this, Auntie.' I couldn't believe it.

Since I found these two, they've both been to meet their natural father's family, and they got on well. The family was glad to know them, and they want to see more of Andrew. Andrew became a mountain climber in the Blue Mountains, and he did exceedingly well. He does well at anything he turns to, and he's a great talker. My sister Leila ended up marrying the brother of their natural father – and their father married another woman from Raukkan. So we used to see him all the time. But their natural father is no longer living. He died some years back.

It was funny, because when I first saw Andrew I said, 'I've seen you before.' You see, Leila and I often went to the market on Saturday mornings years ago. And I'd be sittin' there and I'd say, 'Leila, look at that boy over there. Look, comin' over this way!'

And he'd come over and pass us and we'd say, 'Good morning', and he'd smile. So I said to him all those years later, 'That's the same face.'

And he explained, 'I was working over here for a long time.'

So we sort of passed each other – and yet that feeling was there – that feeling that you knew this boy. It's a funny feeling.

Unfortunately, Mel went down and down and down. He couldn't come to terms with the past – he tried to live in two worlds, and he couldn't do it. He didn't open up to his experiences. We wanted him to. We wanted to get him and sit him down and we wanted to talk to him. But the moment you started talking about it, he clamped up or shut off. Sadly Mel passed on just recently.

Over the years I have met a few more children of the stolen generation and heard what's happened to them – traumatic incidents where there was sexual abuse and stuff like that. Mel just climbed inside himself and that's where he wanted to stay with his drink, you know. It was devastating to realise that it had all hit Mel so hard. With Andrew, he had a different upbringing – maybe because he had another Aboriginal kid with him growing up – whereas Mel was on his own. I said to him that I would have liked to take him somewhere where he could sit down and talk to somone. There has to be more specialised counselling. Otherwise these people today will never come to terms with their past.

We have men here in Adelaide – some who you will find in Victoria Square – who can sit down and tell you of traumatic experiences in their childhood. Victoria Square is where our people get together – some go for drink, but many go to sit there and gather for a yarn. The man I know who remembers his mother sitting down in the middle of the road at Raukkan, screaming for her children, tells you in plain language, 'That was what fucked up my head.' Yet he was still able to go on and have a family himself. You know, there are many men living with memories like that. How can you compensate people for things like that? Some people think that the officers of the day did what they thought was right. All I can say to that is, 'My God, you unfeeling bastards.'

*

When the Inquiry into the Stolen Generation came here to Adelaide, I went in to tell them about my two nephews who had been taken away. I had to go to ACCA – the Aboriginal Child Care office – and they took me to where Mick Dodson was. I hadn't met Mick before, although I'd heard of him on TV and heard people talk about him. I'd met Pat, his brother, once or twice before. But I didn't know what sort of person I'd be meeting in Mick.

When I went in, I didn't know if the information I had would be of any relevance or any use to this Inquiry. But, having found my two nephews, I thought I would go in and tell him my case and what had happened. So I went in and they took me up to this motel room where Mick Dodson was. And I met him, and he said, 'Sit down, have a cup of tea.' So I started telling him the story of how my nephews had been playing together as two little boys on the beach and didn't know they were brothers. And do you know, the man just broke down in tears. He could not believe how these adoptive mothers knew one another, and knew these little boys were brothers, but never said anything. They had played together as children, but never met again till thirty years later. Now, where's the justice in that?

Chapter 16

Reconciliation

In May 1997 I travelled over to Melbourne with Auntie Cherie Watkins and Auntie Maggie Jacobs to the Reconciliation Convention. I was excited because there hadn't been a convention like this before, and I thought I'd never see reconciliation in my time. And I still think that I may not see reconciliation in my time – maybe it'll have to be after I'm gone. But going along gave me some feeling of hope.

On the first day of the conference I met lots of people I have met before on my interstate travels and meetings and seminars over the years. The mere fact that I was meeting up with some of those people was great, because you're all fighting for the same thing. It's good when you can ask people how they got on in their areas and they can ask you the same thing. So going over was full of excitement and fun – but I don't know so much about the fun bit, because in the end the convention turned out to be such an emotional one.

The first day was just generalising and speakers were up there, like Howard, Beazley, Kennett and Kernot. And that was our day – the Ngarrindjeri women's day – to demonstrate. We had taken with us our 'Grandmother's law' banner, and we had our own Ngarrindjeri women's banner. During Howard's speech we got up. Now, this was something that had never been attempted before. We had decided that we would do a silent protest, in the light of what had happened over the Hindmarsh Island Bill. We decided that we would just stand silently and turn our backs on Howard when he spoke, and this would give other people in the audience an idea about what we were protesting against.

So we decided the minute Howard spoke the very first words of his speech, we would stand up in total disrespect for him. We stood there with our backs turned. So I guess if he was able to see the banners from where he was speaking he would have read the words 'Grandmother's Law' and 'Ngarrindjeri women'.

I remember standing there and looking at these people sitting there looking at me, and wondering what they were thinking. There was a white lady sitting straight in front of us, and she started bawling her eyes out, absolutely bawling. And I couldn't believe it. Each time she looked at us she just cried and cried and cried. And then others of us up the back got up and started to stand up, and in about ten minutes quite a lot in that audience stood up with their backs to Howard. By the end of it, three-quarters of us were standing. And I thought, oh, wonderful!

I didn't know what effect it would have on the people – this silent demonstration in standing like that. With a Prime Minister like we've got ... he showed nothing – he was appalling. He banged the table. He must have thought he was talking to some school kids. So we brought him right undone, which was what we had wanted.

We didn't have much time for Beazley either, because of his treatment of us over the Hindmarsh Island issue. He more or less back-pedalled on us, and with other issues regarding Aboriginal people.

But when Cheryl Kernot spoke, it was different. It was really uplifting to have someone get up there and say how much they believed in what the Aboriginal people were trying to do for themselves in this reconciliation process. It was very enlightening to hear someone like Cheryl Kernot get up and say the things she did – and to apologise too for the wrongs that had been done in the past to the stolen generation and so forth. You felt, well, here's someone who actually cares about you.

When we came out, we were down in the foyer, and this fellow came up to us and he said 'Wonderful, you girls. You made that move here today.' And he said, 'It had a big impact on the whole place.' So that was wonderful to hear that.

That afternoon they had the workshops. I attended the women's workshop, which took in issues like education, health and also Hindmarsh Island. We got a lot of support for Hindmarsh Island in there. And the support was great. I didn't think we would get as much support from that group as we did. Auntie Doreen got up and spoke, but I had to leave early because my lift was there. So the next day I was able to get some feedback on it and I found that we got some really good, strong support from that group.

The second day was very, very heavy. You could tell from the feelings of the morning, before the sessions began, that it was going to be a very emotional day. Because that day was for the lost generation, and people spoke from different areas – people who had been taken away told of their feelings and how they had worked to get to know their parents and culture.

That day Evonne Cawley attended, and it was very good to see her there, because in her interview she said that she went because she felt she had to support relatives of hers who she knew had been taken away. So she said going there and listening to the sessions – although she cried and cried – gave her the understanding of what her relatives must have been feeling all those years in trying to find out where their parents were and what had happened to them.

She didn't run a workshop – she just came along and attended in support of the stolen generation. But I think it was good to have someone like her at the conference – to have someone who was known in the sporting world, and known in countries like England and America. Her statement was that she was now teaching her children Aboriginal culture – her culture. She said it was important that they learn of it, and know. She was thrilled to think that she was finding all this out, but it was sad because no matter where you looked there were red eyes. People were so emotionally overcome by what was being said in there.

The whole day was more or less people telling their stories, and people giving papers on the stolen generation. People who had been taken away told of their feelings and how they had tried to go back and meet their families. Actually it was a very traumatic day. You could feel the sadness in the air – everybody wanted to cry – and you did cry, you just couldn't help it. There were all these pent-up feelings that had built up over the years about things that had happened to our kids. There were grown-ups who were sitting around you who had been taken away, and they were shedding these tears continuously. At times you had to get out of there for a break, or you would have sat there so depressed. In fact, at the end of the day there were quite a lot who were depressed. But the whole feeling of the place – both men and women crying together, it was unreal – the passions that people there had for one another.

My cousin Margaret Woods (née Brusnahan) attended the conference. She's a local poet and writer. She was taken away from her mother as a small girl and placed in a State home, Seaforth. From there she was placed in numerous foster homes. She was just one out of the many there who were stolen, and who experienced that traumatised feeling. But it was so sad, because no matter where you looked on the day, there were red eyes. People were so emotionally overcome by what was being said there.

Yes, the stolen generation issues at the conference really opened up the eyes of many people who really didn't know –

particularly white people – that those things did happen to Aboriginal kids. You know, it was unreal. I mean, there was this little girl who was tied to a stake in the back yard and was flogged with the strap. That was outright cruelty – let alone all the other things that happened. That happened in New South Wales, and you can read about it in the stolen generation report, *Bringing Them Home*. I think, reading the report and looking at what some of those kids went through, I just wonder how those kids are now. I wonder how many have been able to come to terms with their past?

And I thought about my nephews – the ones that I had found – and I thought, if only they had been there to hear what was being said. And I wondered how they would feel about it all. Because I know emotionally one of them wouldn't have been able to take it, but the other one would have stood up there in grandeur . . .

*

So now you have read all about my life and about the hard times that a lot of us went through just to survive. If young kids had to live under a system like we did, I don't think they would make it through. It was a very tough system, but it made us tough – we became fighters. When I was young we had to live under two laws: one was the government law of the Protection Board system, and the other was a police law. And if you didn't obey them you were whipped away – shoved off away from your parents and your mission or reserve, and forbidden ever to go back.

A lot of us went through those hard times, but we got through – we became survivors in our own time. We would never be able to do it again. If we had to live that system again today, it would kill a lot of us. How we survived, we do not know. I guess we had a system – but what was that system? We stole; I remember we took from the East End Market – fruit and vegetables or whatever we could find on the truck. We also raided celery patches, tomato patches and heaven knows what. We had to steal to survive, but we didn't beg. That was beneath our dignity.

White people were very privileged in those days, and I can understand why a lot of Aboriginal people who had white skin chose to go for citizenship rights, because they were white, and they could get away with it. But if you were like my shade of colour, you couldn't. You had to stay in there and get put under the Aborigines Act, and do what they told you. Even if you had parents, that made no difference; our lives were even taken out of the hands of our mothers and fathers – the Protection Board had all the say.

Women who married Aboriginal men who had white fathers automatically became white too, and I eventually became one of them. It was like you signed your life away, but at the time it seemed like it was a better thing to do than living under the system.

We always said that a dog had a better life than us. We weren't allowed to open our mouths, and of course we weren't allowed to vote. We were nobody in our own land, aliens in our own country. And today they call a lot of land that's left 'unalienated Crown land'. It's still out there. But in our eyes it still belongs to Aboriginal people.

We had fun times as well as bad times. Coming through all that has helped us survive till now. But a lot of hatred has built up over those years among many of us. There was a time in my life when I really hated – I hated white people. I had to learn not to hate everybody, but to just hate that system and the people who worked in it.

You know, many of us Aboriginal people have never once had a week in our lives when we can sit back and say for the whole week, 'I don't have to worry about anything.' Every day has been a worry to us, and we battle through that. If we're not worrying about where we live, we're worrying about rent, or we're worrying about food. I guess a number of white people are also worrying about the same thing, but there is barely one week when we say 'Oh, I don't care. I don't have to worry this week.' Because that never happens to us. We've got to wonder what we're going to survive on and how we're going to survive the week and get through.

In recent years the Hindmarsh Island affair has been really hurtful to us. What concerns us are all the developments that are likely to take place all over that little island now that the bridge is built, because it's a beautiful little island. Its natural flow of water comes in from the Murray Mouth on the south of the island. Now, years ago, where the natural opening of the Murray Mouth was, you couldn't get near it because of its ferocity. The opening of that mouth was very fierce, but it kept the natural flow of water to the Coorong coming through. That's where we used to camp as children. So what did whiteman do? He went down there with bulldozers and closed up the old mouth and made an opening further down. They also built the four barrages – Goolwa, Mundoo, Ewe Island, and Tauwitchere – to keep the salt water back. It's totally destroyed the Kurrangk and its surrounds for us.

Now you can see that what they did was wrong, because it's thrown the whole natural flow of the Kurrangk right out, as well as the waters around Hindmarsh Island. The Kurrangk is drying up, and if it keeps happening we won't have a Kurrangk any more. Auntie Maggie Jacobs will tell you that all the water there is dirty now, and the beaches have changed – it used to be nice white sand, but we've got none of that now. She can remember what it was like before – and it's all gone. Since those barrages got built they've blocked everything. All the mud has turned into this hard sort of rock. And if they just lift the gates, the fresh water will come through from Lake Alexandrina, and that'll be it. The vegetation all along the Kurrangk will die, and we won't have anything left.

So our fear is that because they've built a bridge to Hindmarsh Island they'll eventually build a bridge across to Mundoo Island. And then they'll want to make a freeway right through down the Kurrangk for all the tourists. That will destroy all that vegetation and everything environmentally. And that's where my sister's ashes lie as well as many other old Ngarrindjeri burial grounds. That whole ninety-mile stretch will be destroyed. So we can't allow that to happen. That land is all that the Ngarrindjeri people have got left, which isn't much, and it's classified as a national park. The Ngarrindjeri have got nothing else but that bit of heritage there at Camp Coorong, near Meningie, and other spots along the Coorong.

What belongs to the Ngarrindjeri nation and what remains of our culture should be left alone. If they respect Aboriginal culture, there shouldn't be any questions or any queries of why. It's only people who are nosy and want to know secret details who cause trouble. So that's why I've called my book *My Side Of The Bridge* – because I wanted to tell you all my side of the argument about the bridge to Hindmarsh Island.

But one thing I'm really happy about is that my daughters have finally come out now and are badgering me and saying, 'Mum, we want to know more.' So that's been good for me – it's been really, really good, because I can sit down and talk to the younger ones now about all sorts of things that are important to me and the Ngarrindjeri women. Because that's how things are handed down. Not, as some people might think, automatically from generation to generation. It's handed down in such a way that a mother or an elder judges whether a particular person is wise enough and ready for the responsibility. My mother knew that my sister was a much wiser person than I, and she knew when it was the right time to tell her certain things. And my sister knew when I was wise enough to be told the stories associated with Hindmarsh Island.

Now people like Pauline Hanson say that Aboriginal people have had too much, and that it's time they got off their butts and did something. Sure, we can get up off our backsides and do things, but then who's always there to put the finish and end to it? The government! We can never get out of their clutches.

And when we hear all this stuff about Aboriginal people getting this and that, they forget what has been done to us as a people over the last two hundred years. The government made a lot of problems for Aboriginal people when they came in and took us over as though they owned us. From day one, we've been under the thumb of the government, and we're still under them today. We can't walk away from them.

We are in a minority and we've become very dependent on the government, because we have so few resources, and all through no fault of our own. Unfortunately this system will stay for a long, long time yet. Autonomy from any government department is like asking for gold, because we know we will never get it – not in my day. I don't think I'll see Aboriginal autonomy for too many programs in my time. They'll always have to be government funded unless we can somehow become financially independent. Maybe if we are compensated for all the land that was stolen from us which we can't claim back, then we will become a little more self-motivated and independent.

We wanted autonomy from the government years ago, but they wouldn't give it. That's because they were scared that if they gave us autonomy to do our own things, they would lose control, and then what would happen? How many people would there be out of work? Look at the big ATSIC offices in Canberra. In every State you look at, who are mostly employed in those buildings? Not Aboriginal people. Most of them are white people. Have you ever been to an ATSIC building? Go in there and have a look, and you won't see too many Aboriginal people working in there.

Applying for money through ATSIC has caused a lot of frustration and disharmony among Aboriginal people. But I suppose that's the way the government wants it to go, because it's keeping a lot of bureaucrats in a job. There's been a lot of ill-feeling because the government of the day slashed ATSIC funding, and that has caused huge problems for Aboriginal people doing good work in many worthwhile programs. So our plight, unfortunately, continues to be in the clutches of the government. But we'll get there. We're survivors and we'll keep climbing the mountain. We've climbed that mountain many times, haven't we?

Looking back at what we've achieved, you've got to remember that we've only been in the broader community for the last thirty-odd years, which is not that long. When I hear criticisms from a lot of whitefellas, I say to them, 'Hey, hang on. We haven't had a very long time to get used to living in a white community that we've never dipped our toes into before. We've had to learn a whole new system, and we've got to learn how to live here with you whitefellas.' So that's why there are problems.

When we left our missions and reserves, and came to live in the towns and cities, we had to learn a lot. I mean, a lot of people have come out to live in the city and have just got browbeaten – they've ended up going back home more broken than when they first came out, because they just didn't understand how to live in the white system. I took this woman to the supermarket when she first came to live in Adelaide, to help her shop – and she ended up rushing into that shop twice a day. I said 'Hey, where are you rushing all the time?'

And she said, 'I'm going shopping.'

So I said, 'Hey! Come on; slow down!'

But she said, 'No! Look at all them whitefellas rushing around!'

And I said to her, 'That's them. That's not for you. Just slow down!'

So you see how the wrong things can be picked up by Aboriginal people who come here to live. They try to live the same lifestyle as the whitefellas, but they're not accustomed to that mode of living.

I think the fault lies with the Department of Aboriginal Affairs. You see, once the referendum came in, they thought, whacko! We'll open the gates and we'll slap 'em all in the city, and they can all have a go at being free citizens. But it didn't work that way. When they lifted the bans that were on us, many of us were already alcoholics. So, with all the new problems that confronted us with our new-found freedom, it didn't create any less alcoholics – in fact, it just created more. And there was no counselling for those who had problems coping psychologically with all the new change. I'm sure if there was there would have been an awful lot of clients!

We had become conditioned, and we had started to believe that we were second-rate citizens. When we entered the theatre in those days, they'd say, 'At the back; not at the front!' So it was like South Africa was with its apartheid regime until recently. We didn't question it, we'd go and sit up in our little box at the back. Same with the train and the bus. So when you get on the train or bus today, where do you go and sit? You sit at the back. It's become a natural response because we were brainwashed to comply with these rules. It was a terrible thing that Aboriginal people had to live and survive under a cruel, heartbreaking regime. Would white people have survived if they had been forced to endure what they made us go through?

So the people who made it difficult for us have a lot to answer for. The people who sat down around some table and made those laws for the Protection Board system must have been Hitler's friends. And I'm pretty sure the people in the department didn't like me much – that's why they took pleasure in having me exempted. If you were a fighter in those days of the Protection Board, they hit you back with an exemption certificate. They'd exempt you for whatever they wanted to. So being an Aboriginal in those days was like having a stigma – but being exempted was also a battle, because it meant you were cut off from your family and your home, and everything else that was dear to you.

But we have a lot of hope for the future, because today we have a lot of Aboriginal people who are out there studying. We've already got a number of Aboriginal lawyers who have come through the university system, as well as a number of medical doctors. It's great, because we're looking at young Aboriginal people now who want to get their degrees or their doctorates in whatever different areas they are studying. Aborigines are finally fighting back by getting themselves educated. We've realised over the years that we have to fight the whiteman on his own terms, even though it's a hard thing to do. A large number have missed out on many, many years of education because of the oppressive Protection Board system. I know there were many Aboriginal people older than myself who were very intelligent and could have done really well if they had been given the opportunity of a good education. But that system thought that we weren't good enough to be educated. The system determined everything for our lives – they even took our thinking away from us!

So at last we're getting somewhere – and it seems today that education for Aboriginal people is the key word. We push it as much as we can to our younger ones, and we push Aboriginal culture as much as we can. They must learn their culture. They must know where they come from. They must know their Dreaming stories. They must know and identify as Aboriginals and be proud to be an Aboriginal.

I always say that I'm proud. I'm proud of what I am and of what I have been able to achieve in my life. And I'm very proud of my colour – no one can knock me for my colour.

Racism doesn't hurt me. But I hate the word and I hate what I hear about racism.

Sometimes I hear these people ringing up on talk-back radio and complaining about their Aboriginal neighbour next door. They say things like, 'No; we don't want them living anywhere near us.' And you also hear of people taking up petitions when they don't want Aboriginal people or organisations establishing themselves in premises in their street. Why? Because they're racist. They are the ones who just like to stir the pot when other people talk of reconciliation.

But such racist things don't rock me now like they used to years ago. Back in those days, when I was treated badly because of my colour, I'd have probably had a go at someone over it. But not today. Now I feel sorry for the person who has got any racism in him or her. Because I think society is like the piano – it's got black and white keys. If you only played the white keys, you'd just have the same old tune in and out. But add a little black to it and the tune goes well. So black and white can and do work together.

And one further thing that I must say is that I believe there is also a great need for harmony between the Ngarrindjeri women and the dissident women who have fallen out over the Hindmarsh Island bridge affair. I must say that I still love the dissident women, as I love all Ngarrindjeri women, despite what happened. And I'm sure somewhere deep inside they love us as well. You know, we were all brought up to love one another. So don't get the idea that we are all bitter enemies. Deep down we've all got hearts, and through our veins beats the same red blood. Somewhere along our bloodlines we are all related.

Obituary

The end of an era with the passing of a beloved matriarch

Veronica Patricia Brodie
Ngarrindjeri and Kaurna Elder
Born: 15 January 1941, Raukkan, South Australia
Died: 3 May 2007, Adelaide

It was a sad day indeed on Thursday 3 May 2007 when South Australia lost one of its true matriarchs – one of its living treasures – with the passing of Auntie Veronica Brodie. This 'giant' of a woman passed away peacefully, surrounded by her devoted family and friends, at the Queen Elizabeth Hospital. This date marks a significant day of mourning for the Kaurna and Ngarrindjeri peoples, who have now lost one of their strongest and most articulate voices. Her passing marks the end of an era. An activist, tireless political campaigner, defender of the disadvantaged, born leader, gifted story teller, public speaker and promoter of reconciliation, Auntie Veronica managed to maintain her rage over the injustices to her people for well over 40 years in her continued struggle for equity for her Indigenous brothers and sisters. But most of all she was a loyal and loving mother, grandmother, sister-girl and friend to all who chose to walk alongside her during her extraordinary life journey. This feisty Nunga mi:mini (Aboriginal woman) packed an awful lot of giving of herself into her all-too-short 66 years of life.

The love and respect felt among the Aboriginal and white community for this trail-blazing activist was demonstrated at

Auntie Veronica's funeral, held at Centennial Park in Adelaide on Friday 11 May. Well over 800 people, from all walks of life, tried to squeeze into the Heysen Chapel to hear Reverend Ken Sumner farewell one of his own in a heart-warming tribute. He spoke in particular of Auntie Veronica's huge capacity to love, and the enormity of the loss of this wonderful woman to the community, particularly those people fortunate enough to have known and befriended her.

Born at Raukkan (formerly Point McLeay Mission) as Veronica Patricia Wilson in 1941 to Dan and Rebecca Wilson, Auntie Veronica was always going to make an impact on all she met. Born premature, and kept alive in a shoebox on the family's wood stove, with a man's handkerchief for a nappy, this determined little bundle of love was destined for great things. She was born the youngest sister of Bert (dec.), Doug (dec.), Leila (dec.) and Graham Wilson, and special sister to Bulla (dec.) and Mickolo (dec.). Following in the footsteps of her politically active grandmother and mother, and her renowned sister Auntie Leila Rankine, it was inevitable that Auntie Veronica was to make her mark. A talented story teller, it was her destiny to share her life story in her autobiography *My Side of the Bridge*. The first book of its kind to emerge from a South Australian Nunga, she reveals with candour and humour what it was like to grow up under the authority of the Aborigines' Protection Board in an era of assimilation. It is hard to believe it was just 40 years ago that the federal government was empowered to legislate against such harsh policies after the success of the May 1967 referendum.

After suffering the injustices of life under the authority of others, Auntie Veronica took on the mantle of activism. With her sister, Auntie Leila, she helped establish the Adelaide Aboriginal Orchestra and the Centre for Aboriginal Studies in Music (CASM) in the 1970s, then in the 1980s the Aboriginal Sobriety group, the 'soup kitchen', Camp Coorong, and an alternative school for Aboriginal students named Warriappendi. Her pioneering efforts continued in the 1990s with her support of the formation of the Aboriginal Elders Village, the Nunga Miminis Women's Shelters, the disability group at Tauondi College, and the Living Kaurna Cultural Centre at Warriparinga. She was soon in constant demand as a speaker at local, national and international events, and was invited to travel to India and Hawai'i. A fierce advocate for the disadvantaged, she was asked to sit on various committees, including the Aboriginal Housing Board and various boards for health and women's issues. She was named NAIDOC Aboriginal Elder of the Year in 2001.

This remarkable woman had an ability to share her love widely. She was like a queen bee who couldn't help but gather copious friends around her, whom she always managed to cajole into becoming her workers for her latest struggle against yet another injustice or fight for a worthy cause. In more recent years, Auntie Veronica was the public face of the campaign against the building of the infamous Hindmarsh Island Bridge, and was vindicated in the Federal Court when the Ngarrindjeri women's claim, that the waters in the Goolwa region have cultural significance, was upheld. Auntie Veronica worked hard to bring her Ngarrindjeri sisters together throughout this unsettling affair. She later founded the Lartelare Glanville Land Action Group, named after her great-grandmother, in an effort to retain just a small pocket of Kaurna land (where her grandmother was born) for her people amidst the recent urban developments along the Port River.

Auntie Veronica is survived by her loyal husband of 45 years, Jimmy Brodie, her four daughters, Margaret, Colleen, Kathleen and Leona, and her stepson Kevin, plus her devoted grandchildren, Troy, Tasha, Bonny, JJ, Samuel, Don Don, Emma and Abbie, and her beloved great-granddaughter Breanah.

Auntie Veronica now rests in peace with the spirits of her Ancestors and with her beloved brothers and sister. Importantly, she rests with her dearly loved only son Michael (dec.), who played a key role, alongside his mum, in the film *Wrong Side of the Road*. May she rest in peace, knowing her legacy will continue in the capable hands of her much loved daughters and grandchildren.

Ngaityo yungandalya, ngaityo yakkanandalya. Padniadlu wadu*
My brothers, my sisters. Let's walk together in harmony.

Written by Mary-Anne Gale (with the Brodie family), May 2007.

---

* A reconciliation gesture in the Kaurna language